F[illegible]ion:

[illegible] NEWTON
at work

EXHIBITION AT CAMBRIDGE UNIVERSITY LIBRARY

9 OCTOBER 2001 – 23 MARCH 2002

Devised and written by Scott Mandelbrote

Cambridge 2001

Published by Cambridge University Library
West Road · Cambridge · CB3 9DR · England

ISBN 0 902205 58 7

A catalogue record for this book is available from the British Library.

Catalogue design: Angela Ashton
University Printing Services, University Press, Cambridge.

Printed by University Printing Services, University Press, Cambridge.

The publication of this catalogue was made possible by the support of the Andrew W. Mellon Foundation.

The web version of this catalogue can be found at:
http://www.lib.cam.ac.uk/Exhibitions/Footprints/

Exhibition design: Jeffery Design

Photography: Les Goodey and Mark Scudder, Cambridge University Library Photography Department

The catalogue illustrations are reproduced by permission of the Syndics of Cambridge University Library, the Wellcome Library, London, and the lenders of the exhibits:

The Syndics of the Fitzwilliam Museum, Cambridge
The Provost and Scholars of King's College, Cambridge
The Museum of the History of Science, University of Oxford
The Master and Scholars of Trinity College, Cambridge
The Whipple Museum of the History of Science, University of Cambridge

PREFACE

The University Library has been at the heart of scholarship in Cambridge for over six hundred years. It is one of the great research libraries of the world, used by scholars from all corners of the globe. The Library's collections have been described in the national press as 'the most accessible collection of literary treasure on this side of the Atlantic'; 'walking around its mile on mile of... corridors, you know you are walking around the world mind.'

These collections, which now occupy over 160 kilometres of shelves, have been built up by a combination of donation and purchase, augmented over the last three-hundred years by the legal deposit privilege. In that time, the Library has acquired many individual items and collections of international significance, but few can match the importance of the purchase, in 2000, of the collection of scientific papers from the library of the Earl of Macclesfield. The Macclesfield Collection was the most important and valuable collection of scientific papers still in private hands in Britain. It documents Sir Isaac Newton's writings and ideas, in letters and manuscripts, on gravitation, calculus, the *Principia mathematica*, optics, chemistry, comets and other subjects. Although widely known for his discovery of universal gravitation, Newton's scientific and intellectual interests were vast, and this range of creative thinking is reflected in these papers.

Since the 'scientific revolution' of the seventeenth century, in which Newton played such a key part, society has been more and more dominated by scientific and technological developments. It would be difficult to find a more striking and graphic illustration of the historical background to this scientific age than the Macclesfield Collection. The collection consists of around 500 manuscript notebooks and a further 500 or so unbound documents. Most of the letters are from the years of Newton's greatest creativity as a mathematician (1664–1672). Though many of the Newton materials have been published in some form, scholars still need to have access to the originals to verify doubtful points in the printed texts. Most of the rest of the collection is completely unknown to scholars, access to it having been restricted in the past. Its acquisition and the provision by the University Library of access to it will lead to new research and publication in this important area.

The collection was offered to the Library for £6,370,000, a price that reflected the extremely active market in scientific manuscripts and books.

In July 2000, the Heritage Lottery Fund provided a grant of £4,790,000, representing 75% of the total purchase price, the maximum the Lottery can offer, but leaving the Library with £1,580,000 to find. Thanks to the generosity of many individuals and institutions, the appeal to raise the balance of the purchase price was spectacularly successful, and before the end of 2000 the Library was able to confirm its purchase of the collection.

The major donors to the appeal are listed elsewhere in this catalogue but I wish to record here our gratitude to all those who supported the campaign, not just those who so generously offered hundreds of thousands of pounds or dollars, but also to those of more moderate means who, nonetheless, believed that the campaign to save this collection was so important that they wanted to do their bit and who sent cheques for £20 or $20. All this support was important and we are very grateful to all who helped.

The career of Sir Isaac Newton (1642–1727) is closely linked with the University of Cambridge. He matriculated at Trinity College, Cambridge in 1661 and became a fellow of Trinity in 1667, occupying the rooms to the north of the Great Gate. He was Lucasian Professor of Mathematics in the University from 1669 to 1701 (the position currently held by Professor Stephen Hawking), and Member of Parliament for the University in 1689–1690 and 1701–1702.

Even before the acquisition of the Macclesfield Collection, Cambridge University Library held by far the most extensive and important group of his scientific papers, chiefly in the Portsmouth Collection, which had been presented to the Library by the fifth Earl of Portsmouth in 1872. The Library also holds manuscripts of Newton's lectures as Lucasian Professor, as well as records of his Cambridge career. There are other smaller collections of Newton's scientific papers in British institutions (notably in the libraries of King's College, Trinity College and the Fitzwilliam Museum in Cambridge, the British Library, the Bodleian Library in Oxford, and the Royal Society) as well as collections of his papers on alchemy, chronology, theology, and other subjects, in various British and foreign libraries.

The Macclesfield and Portsmouth Collections are closely interrelated. Material on some topics, such as the dispute with Leibniz over priority in the invention of the infinitesimal calculus, is spread over both collections and, in some cases, replies to letters in one are to be found in the other. For instance, each collection has correspondence between Newton and John Collins and between Newton and Henry Oldenburg – the Portsmouth Collection contains a letter from Collins to Newton dated 2 July 1672 and the Macclesfield Collection has Newton's replies dated 6 and 8 July. The correspondence of John Flamsteed, Astronomer Royal, in the Macclesfield Collection, complements his correspondence in the Royal Greenwich Observatory Archives, also housed in the University Library.

The acquisition by the University Library of the Macclesfield Collection means that two major sections of the Isaac Newton archive, separated following his death, are now reunited in Cambridge for the benefit of scholars and the public. This important purchase provided the stimulus for this exhibition, celebrating one of Cambridge's greatest minds and the man described as the father of modern mathematics. The exhibition has been devised by Scott Mandelbrote, Newton scholar and fellow of Peterhouse, Cambridge. It draws not just on the Portsmouth and Macclesfield collections but on other parts of the University Library's extensive holdings of scientific material, as well as on collections elsewhere in Cambridge and further afield. Our thanks are due to those institutions which have kindly lent material.

The exhibition is the eighth to be held in the University Library's Exhibition Centre, which was opened in 1998 to provide a wider public than can normally be admitted to the reading rooms with the opportunity of seeing some of the treasures housed within the Library's walls. After the opening exhibition, 'The Great Collections', which was accompanied by a lavishly illustrated book,[1] the series of displays that followed has shown something of the range of the Library's collections, covering such diverse topics as Oliver Cromwell, post-war Germany, maps of Australia, 'time', children's books, and the Armistice. It is fitting that the Library is able to celebrate the acquisition of such a major collection, acquired with the support of the Heritage Lottery Fund, in an exhibition centre, the creation of which was also partly supported by the same fund.

PETER FOX · LIBRARIAN

August 2001

1 *Cambridge University Library: the great collections*, edited by Peter Fox, Cambridge: Cambridge University Press, 1998

ACKNOWLEDGEMENTS

The assistance of the following, both at the time of the acquisition of the Macclesfield Collection and in the preparation of the exhibition and its catalogue is gratefully acknowledged:

Professor Sir Michael Atiyah, David Bell, Dr Jim Bennett, Fiona Duffy, Roger Edgar, Peter Fox, Bamber Gascoigne, Professor Peter Goddard, Professor Tim Gowers, Sir John Guinness, David Hall, Professor Stephen Hawking, Andrew Hunter, Dr Rob Iliffe, Dolores Iorizzo, Peter Jones, Professor Peter Lipton, Dr David McKitterick, Giles Mandelbrote, Scott Mandelbrote, Dr Ros Moad, Dr Tabitta van Nouhuys, Dr Stella Panayotova, Adam Perkins, Dr Simon Pulleyn, Paul Quarrie, Professor Sir Martin Rees, AnneMarie Robinson, Professor Malcolm Schofield, Mark Scudder, Professor Amartya Sen, Harvey Shoolman, Louise Simpson, Dr Steve Snobelen, Dr Liba Taub, Carol Vorderman, Dr Charles Webster, Catriona West, Joan Winterkorn, Joanna Womack, Dr John Young, Dr Patrick Zutshi

The Library is grateful to the following for lending materials to the exhibition:

The Syndics of the Fitzwilliam Museum, Cambridge
The Provost and Scholars of King's College, Cambridge
The Master and Scholars of Trinity College, Cambridge
The Museum of the History of Science, University of Oxford
The Whipple Museum of the History of Science, University of Cambridge

MAJOR DONORS TO THE APPEAL TO ACQUIRE THE MACCLESFIELD COLLECTION:

Heritage Lottery Fund
Mr Malcolm Boston
Mr James H. Brandi
The Dibner Fund
Friends of Cambridge University Library
Friends of the National Libraries
Golden Charitable Trust
The Horace W. Goldsmith Foundation
Mr Gurnee F. Hart
Mr Murray T. Holland
The Fanny and Leo Koerner Charitable Trust
The Andrew W. Mellon Foundation
Mercers' Company
Dr Stuart Morrison
The William Petschek Philanthropic Fund
Mr Robert W. Richardson
Mr John R. Scriven
Thriplow Charitable Trust
Trinity College Cambridge
R.S. Whipple Fund

CONTENTS

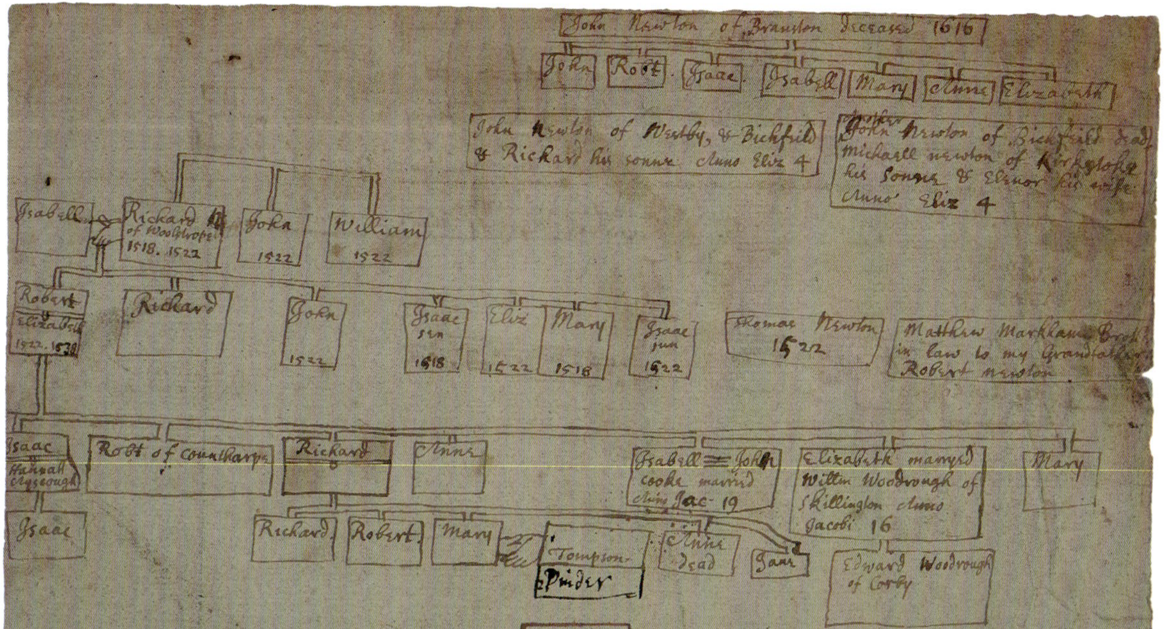

An Ellis built Panton steeple by whom I am akin to Mr Skivard, my Ld & Captaine Skivard my Lady Ellis

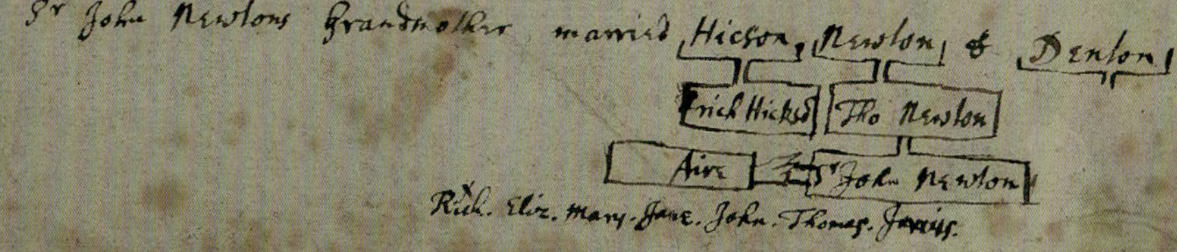

INTRODUCTION

FIGURE 1
A draft of Newton's pedigree, King's College, Cambridge, Keynes Ms. 112/4.

A little before his death, Isaac Newton (1642-1727) is supposed to have remarked, 'I don't know what I may seem to the world, but as to myself, I seem to have been only like a boy playing on the sea-shore and diverting myself in now and then finding a smoother pebble or a prettier shell than ordinary, whilst the great ocean of truth lay all undiscovered before me.'[1] Newton's image of his life's work as a form of childish play was a powerful and enduring one. Along with many of the other tales that collected about him when he was an old man, this saying used personal modesty and understatement as a means to bring home the magnitude of Newton's achievements. It suggested that they were somehow the natural products of genius rather than the fruit of hard mental, and sometimes physical, labour. Another example of this kind of story is the apocryphal account of the fall of an apple in the garden of Newton's family home in Lincolnshire. It again hints that Newton was not like other men and that he possessed a remarkable, intuitive understanding of nature and its laws.

This exhibition has several purposes. The first is to provide an opportunity to display some items that the University Library has recently acquired from the Macclesfield Collection, which was the last major holding of Newton's manuscripts and papers to remain in private hands. A more important aim, however, has been to show the way in which this acquisition complements existing collections in Cambridge libraries and thus how it can help us to understand Isaac Newton. Newton's life, thought, and publications have frequently been written about; the intention of this exhibition is not only to discuss his work but also to examine how he worked.

Anecdotes about picking up pebbles on a beach or watching apples fall from trees were designed in part to obscure the endeavour required for Newton's discoveries. They distanced his ideas from criticism by taking them into the realm of inspiration rather than showing how they developed as a result of tenacity and sustained effort in the face of a problem. The stories of Newton's genius paradoxically conceal what it was that he achieved by removing it from any human context. In order to appreciate Newton's originality and the success of his ideas, it becomes necessary to discover how he came to formulate his thoughts and how he provided proof to his contemporaries that his strange ideas were so often right. This involves removing him from the world of myth, into which his followers assiduously tried to introduce him and where he clearly felt at home by the end of his career. By placing Newton instead in the world of work, it is possible to see how he became a mathematician and natural philosopher through reading and practice, and how, once he had become one, he exceeded the bounds of all but a handful of his contemporaries, through the diversity of his interests as well as the determination with which he pursued them.

In one sense, at least, the anecdotes about Newton may be right. In his early career, Newton's working environment was unusually solitary. Later in life, once he had become both a public figure and a servant of the state, Newton had a reasonably wide circle of acquaintance. He became an attraction sought out by intellectual tourists and curious laymen in a way that had been inconceivable when he was a Cambridge don incapable of holding an audience in his lectures. As a young man, however, Newton knew few people even in the small town of Grantham in Lincolnshire, where he grew up, or the large village of Trinity College, Cambridge, where he studied and worked. Newton initially discovered a world not by exploration or from travellers' tales but through reading and the emulation and extension of what he read. His first, great master was René Descartes and he only emerged from the Frenchman's shadow once he was past his fortieth birthday. Yet the pattern of Newton's reading changed as he grew older. At first, he studied a small number of mathematical and philosophical works very intently. What prompted him to do so is unclear, but the depth of thought that he applied took him further than the conclusions of his authors, although not at first beyond their assumptions. Later, partly as a result of being able to afford more books, he seems almost to have developed the habit of trying to read himself out of any problem that confronted him. This was certainly true of his approach to the theological issues that puzzled him and in many ways it also represented his first entrance into chemical experiment. By the 1690s, he even seemed to be searching for the elusive cause of gravity in the writings of the earliest philosophers.

It would be a mistake to assume that Newton was simply bookish, despite the role that books played in his life. Many of his experiments and observations may have begun life in his reading but it was his outstanding ability at the manipulation of glass prisms and lenses and of metal mirrors that made them a fruitful means of philosophical investigation. More than that, Newton was committed to writing as an active pursuit that helped him to solve questions rather than merely to publish books. Writing introduced Newton to a wider world, through the first correspondence that he developed with John Collins from 1669. But as well as providing new opportunities, correspondence and publication eventually threatened

Newton's independence. They promised constantly to pull him away into unproductive talk or controversy, and in the end they largely won him over to these pursuits. Newton was too reticent ever to be the darling of a literary world, but he could defend his honour with unparalleled cunning and ferocity. Yet although publication helped to create Newton's fame, secrecy defended it. Newton consistently concealed his methods until they had produced definite results and hid his assumptions from investigation by others until they had proved that they could be trusted.

One of Newton's younger contemporaries, the Swiss mathematician Johann Bernoulli, once ruefully remarked that he could identify Newton's hand in a solution to a mathematical problem in the same way that he could identify a lion by its footprint. The traces that allow us to reconstruct part of Newton's world of work consist of the evidence that he left behind of his reading and writing, and through them of his methods and practices. Newton's manuscripts are often hard to interpret, not least because of the difficulty of determining their exact date and hence of understanding their relationship to each other. But they provide a sounder platform from which to regard him than the shifting sands of a mythical beach.

A NOTE ON DATES AND TRANSLATIONS

All dates in this catalogue follow the Julian calendar that was still in use in England throughout Newton's lifetime. I have assumed, however, that each year begins on 1 January, rather than on 25 March.

Many of Newton's works were written in Latin. In general, he has been well served by the translators who have produced English editions of his writings in recent years. Nevertheless, I have normally preferred to offer my own translations in order to bring out particular points that I have wished to make and that the Latin text will support.

1 Joseph Spence, *Observations, Anecdotes and Characters of Books and Men*, ed. James M. Osborn, 2 vols (Oxford, 1966), vol. 1, p. 462.

at 9^h 8' at night.

The length of its tayle was about 11^d being ext[illegible] towards Aldebaran or a little below it paral[illegible] to ye Ecliptick. The tayle now perfectly manif[illegible] it selfe on y^t ~~west~~ east side ~~& y^e * began to cover it selfe, ye cloude being now dissipated~~. It moved northward against ye streame of ye Vortex cutting it [illegible] an angle of about 45^d or 46^d. There was a very bright {haire / beard} round about ye Comet & seemed to bee nothing but bird raying ~~for I co[illegible]~~ from ye center of it for I could not see y^e [illegible] of y^e *.

Dec 28th ye comet was distant from ye bright [illegible] in ye jaw of ye Whaile 8^d 52'. from y^e [illegible] star q in ye Whailes mouth 3^d 43'. Covering y[illegible] twixt ~~[illegible]~~ y^e 3^d & 5^t of y[illegible] with its haire but being [illegible] above it as [illegible] figure. Its ta[illegible] extending to y[illegible] & 4th stars in [illegible] section of y^e [illegible]

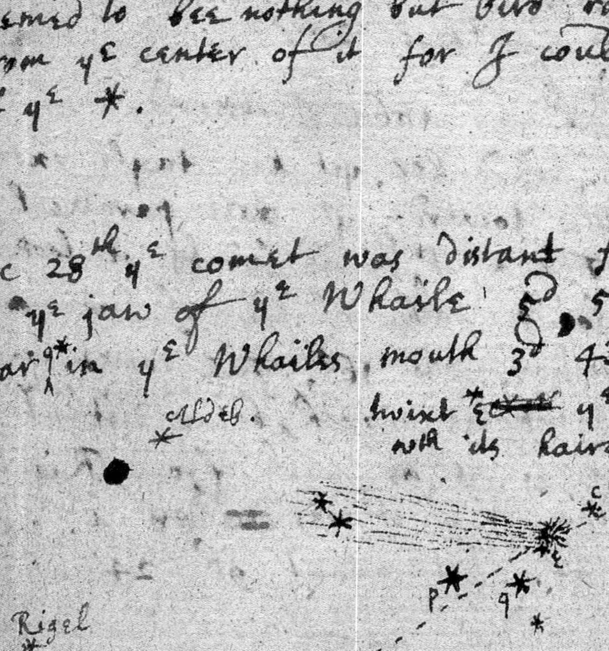

Dec: 29th when 'twas in y^e meridian its alti[illegible] was 44^d 13'. Therefore its declinacon was 6^[illegible] Northward. ~~It passed a little below y^e * c wch below y^e whales eye~~.

Dec: 30th 15 min past 7^h at night The righ[illegible] ascen. of ye Comet was ye same wth y^e * s [illegible]

LEARNING AND TEACHING

FIGURE 2
Newton's first observations of a comet, Ms. Add. 3996, f. 115v.

Newton grew up at Woolsthorpe Manor, Lincolnshire. His family was prosperous, despite the death of Newton's father before his son's birth on Christmas Day 1642. The young Isaac, who showed little interest in tending his mother's flocks, did not have a happy childhood. In 1661, he entered Trinity College, Cambridge, but displayed few signs of exceptional promise until the year 1664, when he embarked on an intensive course of reading and note-taking in contemporary mathematics and natural philosophy. By the following year, when he retreated from Cambridge because of the spread of plague to the city, Newton's curiosity had begun to focus on the mathematical problem of describing curved lines and surfaces and the areas or volumes beneath them. He was also fascinated by philosophical questions associated with colour. At home in Lincolnshire, Newton started to develop answers to these problems. His reading also led him to consider other topics, such as the nature of gravity (with or without the assistance of the apple tree that has been given so much credit for his later discoveries). When he was elected a fellow of Trinity in 1667, Newton was already an accomplished, if unknown, natural philosopher. He soon acquired his first patrons, and, in 1669, he was appointed to succeed Isaac Barrow as Lucasian Professor of Mathematics. He held the post until 1701. Early in 1670, Newton delivered his first lectures. These described his experiments with prisms and set out his new theory of light.

1 KING'S COLLEGE, CAMBRIDGE, KEYNES MS. 112/4
(figure 1 – introduction)
15 × 18.5 cm

This small scrap of paper represents one of several attempts by Newton to establish his ancestry. He eventually decided that he descended from John Newton of Westby, Lincolnshire, whose son, also John Newton, had purchased an estate at Woolsthorpe, near Grantham. Four generations of the family had resided there, before the birth of young Isaac in the manor house that had been bought in 1623 by his grandfather, Robert. They had mostly been buried in the parish church at neighbouring Colsterworth, where Newton himself had been baptised. Newton relied on the monuments and records of this church, together with deeds in his own possession, in drawing up this family tree. Newton's ancestors were solid Lincolnshire husbandmen and yeoman farmers, who had advanced the family's fortunes until they were able to aspire to gentility as lords of the manor. Such aspirations were also apparent in the marriage of Newton's father to Hannah Ayscough, a gentleman's daughter, whose dowry augmented the family's lands and finances. She was the first member of the family to have been educated: before 1642, none of Newton's immediate ancestors had been able to sign his own name and none of them had left any evidence of having owned any books. Newton embarked on a new path for the family in terms of learning, but the recognition that he won was nevertheless an extension of the search for wealth and status that had occupied his ancestors.

The genealogical items that survive among Newton's papers, including this one, mostly date from 1705. On 16 April 1705, Queen Anne knighted Newton in Trinity College, and, on 22 November, he filed his family tree with the College of Arms. Sensitive perhaps to the speed of the advance of his family's fortunes, Newton was keen to emphasise his relationship to Sir John Newton of Thorpe, who entered a submission at the College of Arms in support of his kinsman. Towards the end of his life, however, Newton altered his interpretation of his family's early history, suggesting that his grandfather or great-grandfather had come from East Lothian, arriving in England with James I.

C.W. Foster, 'Sir Isaac Newton's Family', *Reports and Papers of the Architectural Societies of the County of Lincoln, County of York, Archdeaconries of Northampton and Oakham, and County of Leicester*, 39 (1928–9), 1–62; William Stukeley, *Memoirs of Sir Isaac Newton's Life*, ed. A. Hastings White (London, 1936), pp. 27–36; David Brewster, *The Life of Isaac Newton* (London, 1831), pp. 347–58.

Sotheby sale, 14 July 1936, lot 177 (7); purchased by 'Ulysses', possibly the dealer Jacob Schwartz, for £6. The lot was subsequently split. J.M. Keynes eventually acquired parts 7 and 8. Other items from the lot may now be found in the Jewish National and University Library, Jerusalem; the Babson Collection (on deposit in the Dibner Library, Cambridge, Massachusetts), and the Harry Ransom Humanities Research Center, University of Texas, Austin.

2 CAMBRIDGE UNIVERSITY LIBRARY, MS. ADD. 3996, ff. 115v–116r
(figures 2 and 9)
14.2 × 9.5 cm
Bound notebook of 140 leaves

Newton's youthful interest in learning was encouraged by his uncle, William Ayscough, and by the schoolmaster at Grantham, John Stokes. Despite opposition from his mother, who wanted him to stay at home and farm, Newton was admitted to Trinity College, Cambridge, on 5 June 1661, and matriculated on 8 July. His uncle had been educated at Trinity and one of the fellows of the College, Humphrey Babington, was related to a family with whom Newton had lodged while at school in Grantham. Perhaps because of some reluctance of his mother's to waste money on education, perhaps in order to assist Babington, Newton entered Trinity as a sub-sizar, that is a student who was to supplement his income by acting as a servant either for the fellows or for other wealthier students, and who was allowed to pay lower fees for attending lectures.

Although this is not the earliest of Newton's surviving notebooks, it may well be the one that he purchased, together with some ink, on his arrival in Cambridge. Undergraduate education at this time consisted largely of following courses of reading directed by a tutor, in Newton's case Benjamin Pulleyn. These initially focussed on the traditional skills of grammar, logic, and rhetoric. At Cambridge, it was also usual for undergraduates to study ethics, metaphysics, physics, and mathematics. Together with some books that he bought in the early 1660s, this notebook bears witness to Newton's first steps in the Aristotelian curriculum of the early modern university. It is dated on the flyleaf, 'Isaac Newton/ Trin: Coll Cant/ 1661', and contains notes and occasional exercises relating to Newton's reading, compiled in the manner of summarising and glossing recommended by most tutors. Many of these notes are written in the rather crude form of secretary hand that the young Newton practised. They cover his study of Aristotle's *Organon* and Porphyry's *Isagoge*; the scholastic compendium, *Physiologiae peripateticae*, by Joannes Magirus; Aristotle's *Ethics* and the *Ethica* of Eustachius of St Paul; the *Axiomata* of Daniel Stahl, which introduced him to Aristotelian metaphysics, and, finally, a text-book of rhetoric by the great humanist scholar, Gerardus Joannes Vossius.

By about the beginning of 1664, Newton's writing had matured into the neat, if slightly spindly, italic hand that he would continue to develop over the rest of his life. His reading and thinking had also taken a new course, albeit one that was promoted by many of the best tutors in contemporary Cambridge. Newton had begun to reflect for himself on the metaphysical and natural philosophical terms and concepts deployed by the scholastic authors that he had been studying. Prompted perhaps by the scholarship to which he was elected in April 1664, Newton had started to read for himself both in the classical sources and commentaries and in contemporary philosophical and scientific writing, notably the works of Walter Charleton and René Descartes. Within the confines of a traditional commonplace book, and deploying many of the categories of renaissance philosophy, Newton had thus embarked through reading on his career as a mechanical, and eventually experimental, philosopher. Quoting portentously from Charleton, he headed his remarks 'Amicus Plato amicus Aristoteles magis amica veritas' (Plato is my friend, Aristotle is my friend, but my greatest friend is truth).

Among the works of the new philosophy with which Newton became acquainted were several dealing with comets. The observation and study of comets was important for natural philosophers since their motion raised questions about the orderly structure of the heavens and the relationship between celestial and terrestrial matter. A list of books that Newton made at the back of this notebook included several of the works that had helped to make the study of comets controversial, notably the *Descriptio cometae* (Leiden, 1619) of the Dutch mathematician, Willebrord Snell, which had analysed the comet of winter 1618–19, as well as tracts by William, Landgrave of Hesse-Cassel, on the comet of 1585, and by the Copernican astronomer, Christopher Rothmann. Newton transcribed tables of the motion of the comets of 1585 and 1618 from Snell. He also noted the appearance of a comet in early December 1664, going on to describe his own observations 'On fryday before midnight Decembr. 23d 1664'.

The pages that are displayed show Newton's continued observations of the comet on 24, 27, 28, 29, and 30 December 1664 and between 1 and 23 January 1665. They include a diagram to illustrate the relative position of the comet with reference to the location of the stars, for which Newton based himself on Vincent Wing's publication (1651) of the catalogue of Tycho Brahe. Newton's descriptions of the comet were not always clear, and his initial attempt to track its movements by comparison with those of the moon displayed his ignorance of the limits of contemporary astronomical knowledge. But the excitement of seeing for the first time 'a Comet whose rays were round her, yet her tayle extended it selfe a little towards [the] east' was clear. Newton had seen with his own eyes that the Aristotelian distinction between comets with rays and comets with tails could not be sustained. Through his reading of Descartes, Newton was also aware of contemporary ideas that the appearance of the comet's tail might simply be an optical phenomenon. He had realised the potential of comets as exemplars of celestial motion. Yet, although his observations proved to be reliable, there is little evidence that Newton's early interest in comets was sustained. He made a few further notes on a new comet in 1665 but seems not to have been concerned by the dispute between the French astronomer Adrien Auzout and his rival from Danzig, Johannes Hevelius, over their observation of the comets of 1664 and 1665.

J.E. McGuire and Martin Tamny (eds), *Certain Philosophical Questions: Newton's Trinity Notebook* (Cambridge, 1983), especially pp. 296–304; A. Rupert Hall, 'Sir Isaac Newton's Note-book, 1661–1665', *The Cambridge Historical Journal*, 9 (1948), 239–50; D.E. Smith, 'Two Unpublished Documents of Sir Isaac Newton', in W.J. Greenstreet (ed.), *Isaac Newton 1642–1727* (London, 1927), pp. 16–34; Richard S. Westfall, *Never at Rest. A Biography of Isaac Newton* (Cambridge, 1980), pp. 66–104; William T. Costello, SJ, *The Scholastic Curriculum at Early Seventeenth-Century Cambridge* (Cambridge, Mass., 1958); Tabitta van Nouhuys, *The Age of Two-Faced Janus* (Leiden, 1998); Gary W. Kronk, *Cometography*, volume 1 (Cambridge, 1999), pp. 350–7.

Assessed 'Not fit to be printed' on behalf of Newton's executors by Thomas Pellet (25 September 1727); presented to Cambridge University Library by the fifth Earl of Portsmouth. See *A Catalogue of the Portsmouth Collection of Books and Papers written by or belonging to Sir Isaac Newton* (Cambridge, 1888), p. 47. Exhibited in 1987: 'The Making of Newton's "Principia" (1664–1687)', case 1, items 1–3.

3 FITZWILLIAM MUSEUM, CAMBRIDGE, MS. 1–1936, ff. 6v–7r

12.1 × 7.1 cm

Bound notebook of 118 leaves

Newton paid 8d. for this pocket-book and seems to have begun using it from what is now the back, entering the alphabet in Hebrew and the meanings of some words under the heading 'Nova cubi Haebraei Tabella'. This is among the earliest evidence that Newton attempted to learn the language of the Old Testament in a serious way. The testimony of his later theological writings, however, suggests that, although he mastered the alphabet and some grammatical rudiments, he remained largely dependent on Latin translations for his knowledge of works written in Hebrew. Among Newton's contemporaries, especially those from godly backgrounds, it was not uncommon to try to add some knowledge of Hebrew to the Greek that was acquired as a second language at grammar school and the Latin that was ubiquitous in learned culture. Some indication of the nature of Newton's own upbringing and of his youthful piety may be gleaned from the shorthand notes that he entered in this pocket-book 'Before Whitsunday 1662'. They consisted of a numbered list of sins, such as the godly were supposed to draw up for self-examination, including transgressions such as 'Using the word "God" openly'; 'Squirting water on Thy day'; 'Putting a pin in John Keys hat on Thy day to pick him', or 'Caring for worldly things more than God'. They gave indications of the similarity of Newton's beliefs and behaviour to the attitudes of many provincial puritans. Already, the nineteen-year-old Newton suggested the obsession with the power and severity of God the Father that would later become a focus for his religious beliefs: 'Not loving Thee for Thy self'; 'Not fearing Thee so as not to offend Thee'. Yet he also displayed more conventional signs of godly anxiety about his failure to keep his 'covenant' with God through the pranks, quarrels, and petty thefts of a rural childhood or of undergraduate banter, as well as through absence from or inattentiveness at worship, or the reading of vulgar, best-selling chapbooks such as the neo-chivalric romance, *The Seven Champions of Christendom*.

Newton appears to have abandoned this pocket-book for a time after 1662, since, to judge both by handwriting and content, the rest of the entries in it were written from the summer of 1664 to the autumn of 1668. Most of these notes concern mathematical problems, for example methods of describing curves and of analysing their properties, and reveal Newton's growing familiarity with contemporary mathematics, in particular geometry. They draw on his reading of the *Clavis mathematicae* (third edition, 1652) of the early seventeenth-century English mathematician, William Oughtred, and more especially on his knowledge of the commentaries and exercises of Frans van Schooten (1615–60). Van Schooten, who was a professor of mathematics at Leiden University in the Netherlands, was also one of the most successful popularisers of the *Geometria* of Descartes. Newton probably encountered this work for the first time through an edition of a Latin translation published by van Schooten in 1649. He soon owned the enlarged edition that van Schooten published between 1659 and 1661 (see catalogue number 31), in which Descartes' work was supported by the algebra of François Viète. This volume also contained the *Elementa curvarum* of the Dutch mathematician and statesman, Jan de Witt, who had been a pupil of Descartes' friend and collaborator, Isaac Beeckman. Newton's working in this pocket-book depends in places on constructions derived from de Witt. Many years later, in a paper sent to Richard Bentley explaining what mathematical reading was necessary in order to understand the *Principia*, Newton urged his disciple to begin by consulting de Witt and the other materials printed by van Schooten in his edition of Descartes.

At some point after he began using it for mathematical purposes, Newton also started to enter accounts in this pocket-book. These are written on the blank pages left over once Newton had marked up the bulk of the pocket-book for the calculation of sine tables. The first entry is dated 23 May 1665 and the accounts then continue until April 1669. They are of considerable interest since they cover the years in which Newton, who took his BA in 1665, ceased to be a student and became a natural philosopher in his own right. In particular, they reveal his expenditure on the tools and instruments necessary for serious work in optics and the widening scope of his reading in contemporary natural philosophy. They also illustrate the mundane expenditures of Newton's life at Cambridge and the more significant purchases associated with the taking of his MA degree (7 July 1668) and his election first to a minor fellowship (2 October 1667) and then to a major fellowship (7 July 1668) at Trinity. For much of the period described by the accounts, Newton was resident at Woolsthorpe, where he fled in summer 1665 in order to escape the plague in Cambridge. He seems to have remained there until late March 1666, returning between June 1666 and April 1667 and again between December 1667 and early February 1668. These accounts demonstrate Newton's continuing financial dependence on his mother, until he began receiving dividends as a fellow of Trinity in 1668. Finally, they provide information about Newton's first visit to London, between 5 August and 28 September 1668, and about the purchase in 1669 of books and equipment for his new interest in alchemical research.

Richard S. Westfall, 'Short-Writing and the State of Newton's Conscience, 1662', *Notes and Records of the Royal Society of London*, 17 (1962), 10–16; D.T. Whiteside (ed.), *The Mathematical Papers of Isaac Newton*, 8 vols (Cambridge, 1967–81), vol. 1, 15–45; H. W. Turnbull, J.F. Scott, A.R. Hall and Laura Tilling (eds), *The Correspondence of Isaac Newton*, 7 vols (Cambridge, 1959–77), vol. 3, 155–6; D. J. Struik, *Het land van Stevin en Huygens* (Nijmegen, 1979), pp. 90–5; [John Taylor], *Catalogue of the Newton Papers Sold by Order of Viscount Lymington* (London, 1936), pp. 52–3; Sir David Brewster, *Memoirs of the Life, Writings, and Discoveries of Sir Isaac Newton*, 2 vols (Edinburgh, 1855), vol. 1, 31–3.

Assessed 'Not fit to be printed' on behalf of Newton's executors by Thomas Pellet (25 September 1727). Collated against the text printed in Brewster's *Memoirs* by H.R. Luard (24 December 1873); entered in *A Catalogue of the Portsmouth Collection of Books and Papers written by or belonging to Sir Isaac Newton* (Cambridge, 1888), p. 48. Sotheby sale, 14 July 1936, lot 210; purchased by Maggs Brothers for £180. Presented to the Fitzwilliam by the Friends of the Museum (with the assistance of Sir Thomas Barlow), July 1936. Exhibited November 1973–January 1974: Michael Jaffe, *The European Fame of Isaac Newton* (Cambridge, 1974), p. 15.

4 ISAAC BARROW (ED.), *Euclidis elementorum libri xv. breviter demonstrati* (Cambridge, 1655)

(figure 3)

12°: A–2G[4]

13.5 × 7.5 cm

Trinity College Library, Cambridge, NQ 16/201

When Newton was a candidate for a scholarship at Trinity in April 1664, he was sent to be examined by the recently appointed Lucasian Professor of Mathematics, Isaac Barrow (1630–77). Barrow supposedly questioned him about Euclid, whose writings Newton had at that point neglected. Barrow was himself the editor of a pioneering edition of Euclid, prepared at first to assist him in teaching mathematics to Trinity undergraduates in the early 1650s. This edition deployed the system of mathematical symbols that William Oughtred had developed to clarify and simplify Euclid's text. Barrow's work displayed his reverence for the geometry of the ancients, as well as his skill in explanation, since it treated the whole of Euclid's *Elements* in a very brief book suitable for students. It was an immediate success when it appeared in February 1656 and it continued to be used very widely as a textbook throughout the later seventeenth century, although some readers felt that its brevity rendered it too obscure for those who were not already competent in geometry. Yet in the words of one student reader, Roger North (1651–1734), 'the forty-seventh proposition, which is that in all [right angled] triangles the square of the greater [side] is equal to those of the two others... entered me alive, as I may say, and I digested it with great satisfaction, and having got Barrow, which is much the best, I launched farther and made myself master of so much as served to common practical geometry...'

In 1657, Barrow published a second work on Euclid, *Euclidis data succincte demonstrata*, which he had written in 1654. This is often found bound up with his earlier edition of the *Elements*, as is the case with Newton's copy, which is on display here. It seems slightly implausible that the young Newton really had so little acquaintance with Euclid as the story about his first meeting with Barrow implies. Nevertheless, the handwriting of Newton's annotations in this standard textbook suggests that he may well have turned to a closer study of Euclid in about 1664. The annotations themselves are not particularly profound. Many of them are fairly trivial corrections, additions, or supplementary proofs, some of which derive from Oughtred. Even the fullest notes, which seem to be the product of a second, more exhaustive reading of the text, are largely explanatory. The most remarkable of these is the one that occurs at proposition XVIII of book X. After he had become Lucasian Professor in his own right, Newton also prepared exercises or lectures based on the second book of Barrow's edition of the *Elements*.

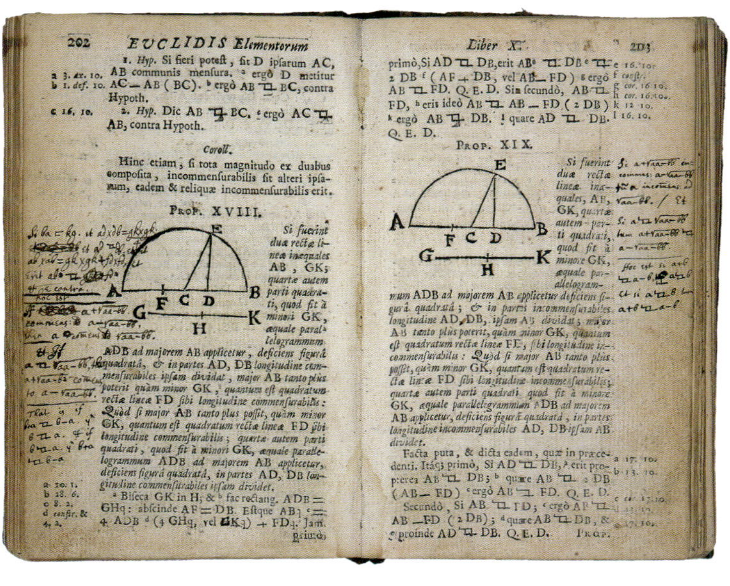

FIGURE 3
Newton's annotations to Isaac Barrow's edition of Euclid, Trinity College, Cambridge, NQ 16/201, pp. 202–3.

Whatever his first impressions, Barrow later formed a much more favourable view of Newton. He received aid from Newton in the preparation of his lectures for the press in 1669 and 1670, and presented Newton with a copy of the finished publication on 7 July 1670 (see catalogue number 32). He also began to publicise Newton's abilities during those years, especially in letters that he wrote to John Collins (see catalogue number 38), who was then helping to see Barrow's lectures through the press in London. With Barrow's encouragement, in 1669, Newton sent his tract 'De analysi' to Collins, revealing some of the work that he had been doing on infinite series during the previous couple of years.

John Harrison, *The Library of Isaac Newton* (Cambridge, 1978), pp. 51, 94–5, 139–40; D.T. Whiteside (ed.), *The Mathematical Papers of Isaac Newton*, 8 vols (Cambridge, 1967–81), vol. 1, p. 12; vol. 3, pp. 389, 402–7; Mordechai Feingold, 'Isaac Barrow: divine, scholar, mathematician', in Feingold (ed.), *Before Newton. The Life and Times of Isaac Barrow* (Cambridge, 1990), pp. 1–104, especially pp. 40–7; Augustus Jessopp (ed.), *The Autobiography of the Hon. Roger North* (London, 1887), p. 16; H. Zeitlinger, 'A Newton Bibliography', in W.J. Greenstreet (ed.), *Isaac Newton 1642–1727* (London, 1927), pp. 148–70, especially pp. 168–70.

Listed by the booksellers who appraised Newton's library for his executors; bought with the rest of the library by John Huggins in 1727. Bookplate of Charles Huggins. Bookplate of James Musgrave, with shelfmark E3–23. Presumed sold at Thame Park, 13–15 January 1920. Sold at Sotheby's, 20 April 1926, lot 597, purchased by Sotheran & Co. for 5s. Advertised in Sotheran's catalogues 804 (1927) and 828 (1931) at £500. Purchased for £500 by the Pilgrim Trust and presented to Trinity College, Cambridge, on 30 October 1943.

5 CAMBRIDGE UNIVERSITY ARCHIVES, O.XIV.106

(figure 4)

43.5 × 66.5

In 1669, Isaac Barrow resigned the Lucasian Chair of Mathematics, perhaps in order to devote more time to his calling as a divine. Newton was appointed as his successor on 29 October 1669, almost certainly as a result of patronage from Barrow. The professorship had been endowed by the will of Henry Lucas, who died in 1663, and carried a stipend of around £100 per annum. The holder of the chair was allowed to retain the income from his College fellowship and to hold ecclesiastical appointments provided that they required no pastoral duties. He was not permitted to hold College office, however. The limits implied in these terms may also explain why Barrow, who subsequently became a royal chaplain and Master of Trinity, resigned his appointment. They

FIGURE 4
Letters patent granting the Lucasian Professor of Mathematics dispensation from taking holy orders, University Archives, O.XIV.106.

were nevertheless acceptable to Newton. Unfortunately, by 1675, the requirement of Newton's College that he take holy orders, like all other fellows of seven years' standing, had become intolerable to him. In around 1673, Newton had begun to have doubts about orthodox teaching concerning the Holy Trinity, in particular believing that God the Father was different from and superior to Christ and the Holy Ghost. Consequently, he was no longer able to contemplate orders in the Church of England, whose Thirty-Nine Articles affirmed the doctrine of the Trinity.

There was, however, a way for Newton to avoid having to resign his fellowship. This was to receive a royal dispensation. Newton made several unsuccessful attempts to seek patronage to this end during 1674. It seems that, in the end, Barrow came to his rescue and bent the ear of the King. Newton was allowed to submit a draft for a patent that would allow the Lucasian Professor to hold a College fellowship without taking orders. He submitted his draft on 2 March 1675, and, on 27 April 1675, the letters patent displayed here were issued under the broad seal, according almost exactly to Newton's own wording.

Richard S. Westfall, *Never at Rest. A Biography of Isaac Newton* (Cambridge, 1980), pp. 206–8, 330–4; J. Edleston (ed.), *Correspondence of Sir Isaac Newton and Professor Cotes* (London, 1850), pp. xlix-l.

6 CAMBRIDGE UNIVERSITY LIBRARY, MS. ADD. 4002, pp. 4–5

(figure 5)
23.1 × 17.3 cm
Bound quarto notebook of 182 leaves

Following his appointment as Lucasian Professor, Newton chose to use his first series of lectures as a vehicle to expound the new theory of light and colours that he had been developing since the mid-1660s. Rejecting the scholastic distinction between real and apparent colours, Newton had taken up the ideas of Descartes and of Robert Boyle in writing an essay 'Of Colours' (see catalogue number 11). He accepted the notion that colour was produced by the modification of light as it falls on a particular body and, by 1666, had begun to understand the phenomenon of refraction. This led him into further work on geometrical optics, a topic that was also being considered extensively by Barrow in his own Lucasian lectures that Newton would later help to prepare for publication.

As Lucasian Professor, Newton was required to deliver one lecture, lasting perhaps an hour, each week during term and to submit at least ten such lectures to the Vice-Chancellor annually for deposit in the University Library. Newton eventually presented a copy of his optical lectures to the University on 21 October 1674, by which time the *Optica* consisted of thirty-one lectures and was divided into two parts. These lectures had supposedly been delivered between January 1670 and the

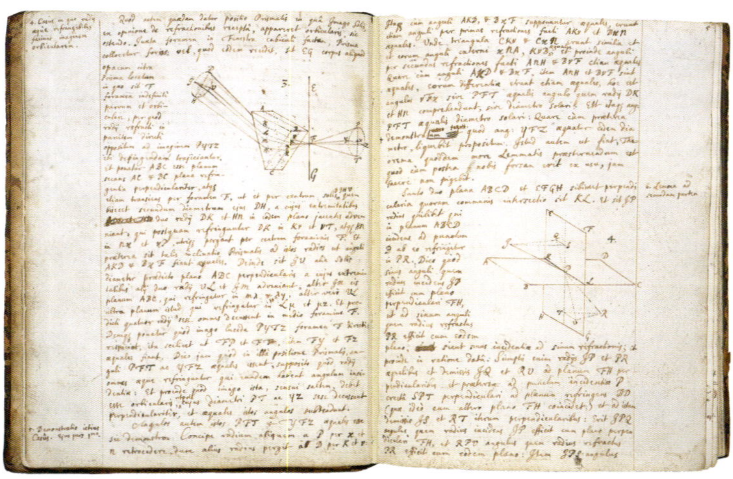

FIGURE 5
Experiments with a prism from Newton's first Lucasian lectures, Ms. Add. 4002, pp. 4–5.

end of Michaelmas Term 1672. By 1674, Newton had revealed many of his optical discoveries in letters sent to the secretary of the Royal Society, Henry Oldenburg, and published in his journal, the *Philosophical Transactions*. He had already suggested to others, including Barrow and Collins, that he was preparing the text of his lectures for publication. However, by the autumn of 1674, Newton had developed a deep distrust of printed communications as a means of securing credit and publicity for his scientific work. As a result, a manuscript copy of his lectures was deposited in Cambridge and, for more than a decade and a half, he abandoned his plans to publish them.

Newton nevertheless retained another manuscript of his lectures among his own papers. This was also a fair copy, preserved in the notebook on display here. It differed from the manuscript that he deposited in the University Library in a number of particulars and was also substantially shorter than it. It appears to have been completed in this form by about October 1671, after which Newton seems to have set it aside entirely and to have rearranged the order of presentation of his material. Nevertheless, this notebook contained almost all the major elements of Newton's optical lectures and represented the principal fruit of his research about the properties of light, conducted in the second half of the 1660s. Eighteen lectures were written out on 128 numbered pages and a different order of delivery was claimed from that in the later *Optica*. Both manuscripts, however, agree that the lectures began in January 1670.

The opening lecture, part of which is illustrated here, laid the foundations for all that would follow by showing that sunlight consists of rays that differ in their degree of refrangibility. In this lecture, Newton deployed experiments with a prism to demonstrate his ideas. Having found that a narrow beam of sunlight passed through a prism produces an elongated spectrum, he explained that it was indeed possible to achieve results that upheld the conventional view of refraction. Adherents of this theory argued that light rays should be refracted equally so that the sun's light would produce a circular image on passing through a prism. But Newton pointed out that this was a special case, whose properties he then investigated. He then went on in his second lecture to describe the shape of the spectrum created by his experiments and to observe that the same results could be achieved through considering the spectrum of Venus or of stars other than the sun.

These ideas were later taken up by Newton in his *Opticks* (1704). However, the difference between his treatment of them there and in these lectures was sufficient to prompt his executors to publish first an English translation (1728) and then a Latin edition edited by David Gregory (1729), both based on the manuscript of the *Optica*.

Alan E. Shapiro (ed.), *The Optical Papers of Isaac Newton*, vol. 1 (Cambridge, 1984), 1–81, especially pp. 52–7; D.T. Whiteside (ed.), *The Unpublished First Version of Isaac Newton's Cambridge Lectures on Optics 1670–1672* (Cambridge, 1973); Richard S. Westfall, 'Newton's Reply to Hooke and the Theory of Colours', *Isis*, 54 (1963), 82–96; J. A. Lohne, 'Isaac Newton: The Rise of a Scientist 1661–1671', *Notes and Records of the Royal Society of London*, 20 (1965), 125–39; Maurizio Mamiani, *Isaac Newton, filosofo della natura. Le lezioni giovanili di ottica e la genesi del metodo newtoniano* (Florence, 1976).

Assessed 'Not fit to be printed' on behalf of Newton's executors by Thomas Pellet (25 September 1727); presented to Cambridge University Library by the fifth Earl of Portsmouth. See *A Catalogue of the Portsmouth Collection of Books and Papers written by or belonging to Sir Isaac Newton* (Cambridge, 1888), p. 48.

7 CAMBRIDGE UNIVERSITY LIBRARY, MS. Dd. 4. 18, f. 1r
30.1 × 19.3 cm
26 folio leaves in a modern binding

The five lectures contained in this manuscript, under the title 'De motu Corporum Liber [secundus]', were supposedly delivered by Newton during Michaelmas Term 1687, beginning on 29 September, and then duly deposited in the University Library. They have been copied from a longer version of the text, which was probably written in the months before autumn 1685. Newton's heirs published the full text in 1728 as an addition to the *Principia*, under the title *De mundi systemate*.

The manuscript is not, however, the text of lectures actually delivered by Newton but rather a copy of part of a draft for Book III of the *Principia* that Newton later rejected. Passages that were later corrected by Newton are in places omitted entirely in this copy. It is thus principally interesting as an example of the manner in which Newton fulfilled the requirement that, as Lucasian Professor, he deliver suitable lectures and deposit copies of them in the University Library. It also provides an illustration of the collaboration between Newton and his amanuensis, Humphrey Newton. Newton had arranged for Humphrey, who was not related to him, to come up to Cambridge from the grammar school in Grantham either in 1683 or 1684. Humphrey Newton then served as

Isaac Newton's amanuensis for five years, during which he may also have been his sizar, although Humphrey appears not to have been admitted as a member of Trinity College. Many of Newton's compositions during this period survive in drafts written by Humphrey Newton, including both versions of 'De motu corporum liber secundus'. The most notable of these works is the manuscript from which the text of the *Principia* was printed. Humphrey Newton later returned to Grantham, where he practised as 'a physician and manmidwife' according to William Stukeley, and was still alive in 1728. The reminiscences of his master that he related to Stukeley and John Conduitt are the source for many of the stories of Newton's absent-mindedness as well as providing evidence for the pattern of Newton's life in College and his intellectual activity during the late 1680s.

I. Bernard Cohen, *Introduction to Newton's 'Principia'* (Cambridge, 1971), pp. 109–15, 299–309; Richard S. Westfall, *Never at Rest. A Biography of Isaac Newton* (Cambridge, 1980), pp. 343–4; Cambridge University Library, Ms. Add. 3990; William Stukeley, *Memoirs of Sir Isaac Newton's Life*, ed. A. Hastings White (London, 1936), p. 22; King's College, Cambridge, Keynes Ms. 135. Exhibited in 1987: 'The Making of Newton's "Principia" (1664–1687)', case 6, item 2.

8 CAMBRIDGE UNIVERSITY LIBRARY, MS. ADD. 4005, ff. 14–15
29 × 18.2 cm

This brief document, headed 'Of educating Youth in the Universities', probably dates from the 1690s, when Newton was consulted on appointments and practices at both the universities of Oxford and Cambridge and at Christ's Hospital in London. It draws on Newton's own educational experience in places, and certainly reflects his interest in particular topics of natural philosophy. The programme of study that Newton recommends is fairly conservative: as a young man, he would certainly have recognised a mathematical education grounded on 'some easy & usefull practicall things, then Euclid, Sphericks, the projections of the Sphere, the construction of Mapps, Trigonometry, Astronomy, Opticks, Musick, Algebra...' The course that he suggested in philosophy concentrates on many of the topics that he had himself considered as a student and recorded in his commonplace book (see catalogue number 2): 'time, space, body, place, motion & its laws, force, mechanical powers, gravity & its laws, Hydrostaticks, Projectiles solid & fluid, circular motions & [the] forces relating to them'. Nevertheless, these were precisely the areas of natural philosophy that had been revolutionised by Newton's own published work in the *Principia*. However, while it is tempting therefore to assume that Newton intended his own writings to become the basis of undergraduate instruction, one should perhaps remember that Newton was known in Cambridge as 'the man who has writt a book that neither he nor any one else understands'. Most of the relatively few people who could claim to understand the *Principia* during the 1690s were either distinguished natural philosophers in their own right or individuals close to its author who were able to ask him for advice. Yet Newton's insistence in this document that mathematical learning should underpin later investigations in natural philosophy is still remarkable.

The most unusual aspects of Newton's scheme, however, relate to the administration of learning. Not only did he suggest that Colleges should employ designated people to serve as lecturers in subjects like mathematics or philosophy, in addition to the role played by undergraduate tutors, but he also specified the terms under which they should serve. He was equally thorough concerning the duties of tutors and the fees that they might charge their students. Finally, Newton was explicit in condemning what he saw as a continuing legacy of Roman Catholic error. This was the practice of forcing College fellows to swear that they would take orders or uphold the established Church. He attacked the perjury that he believed to be the inevitable result of this behaviour and insisted that others should be allowed the religious toleration that he had himself enjoyed: 'No oaths of office to be imposed on [the] Lecturers'.

A. Rupert Hall and Marie Boas Hall (eds), *Unpublished Scientific Papers of Isaac Newton* (Cambridge, 1962), pp. 369–73; James L. Axtell, 'Locke, Newton and the Two Cultures' in John W. Yolton (ed.), *John Locke: Problems and Perspectives* (Cambridge, 1969), pp. 165–82; King's College, Cambridge, Keynes Ms. 130.5, number 2.

Presented to Cambridge University Library by the fifth Earl of Portsmouth. See *A Catalogue of the Portsmouth Collection of Books and Papers written by or belonging to Sir Isaac Newton* (Cambridge, 1888), p. 49.

[Dating to the 1690s confirmed from the watermark (fleur de lys/HD)]

A PRIVATE SCHOLAR AND A PUBLIC SERVANT

During his years in Cambridge, the focus of Newton's activities shifted several times. His initial enthusiasm for geometry, optics, and the making of instruments developed into a passion for alchemical experiment during the 1670s. His growing unease about the doctrines of the Church of England forced him to contemplate giving up his life at Cambridge, until he received royal dispensation to hold his professorship without taking holy orders. It also led him to investigate the beliefs of the early Church, and, in the 1680s, to work intensively on the historical problem of the origin of religion. By then, his ideas about matter and motion were beginning to take shape. Behind these changes of interest lay changes in what Newton was reading. As he built up his library and constructed his own laboratory, the method of his studies also altered. Yet Newton's interests remained those of a solitary intellectual, and it took the political upheaval of the Glorious Revolution in 1688, as well as the publication of the *Principia*, to make him into a public figure. Newton supported the Revolution and was elected as the MP for Cambridge University straight after it. His new patrons soon found ways for him to leave the Fens for good, and Newton effectively gave up the duties of his chair in 1696 when he moved to London permanently to become Warden of the Mint.

9 CAMBRIDGE UNIVERSITY LIBRARY, MS. ADD. 4000, ff. 26v–27r
(figure 6)
14.7 × 9 cm
Bound notebook of 164 leaves (originally 166)

Newton appears to have begun using this notebook in the winter of 1663–4 and to have written in it extensively over the next two or three years. It contains notes on his mathematical and geometrical reading, drawn from van Schooten's *Exercitationum mathematicarum* (Leiden,

1657) and from his edition of the works of Viète (Leiden, 1646), as well as from the writings of the Oxford mathematician, John Wallis. Newton was particularly interested in Wallis' *Arithmetica infinitorum* (included in his *Opera mathematica* of 1656–7), in which problems of mathematical methods of reasoning about the quadrature of areas and volumes through consideration of their indivisible elements of line and surface were set out. This notebook also contains evidence of the development of Newton's own mathematical skill in this period, especially his study of infinite series and development of the binomial theorem, the evolution of the differential calculus, and its application to the problem of quadratures and integration. Although Newton had been inspired in his mathematical work on curved lines and surfaces by reading Wallis and by listening to the lectures that Barrow delivered in 1664, his knowledge of Descartes' geometry was also critical in these discoveries.

One of the later entries in this notebook derives from Newton's knowledge of Descartes' *La dioptrique*, which Newton probably read in a Latin edition published at Paris in 1656. By September 1664, Newton had learned about the sine law of refraction through his reading of Descartes' works, and, in the winter of 1665–6, he investigated

FIGURE 6
Shaping a wheel for the grinding of lenses, Ms. Add. 4000, f. 26v.

FIGURE 7
A copy of Newton's essay 'Of Refractions', from the Macclesfield Collection.

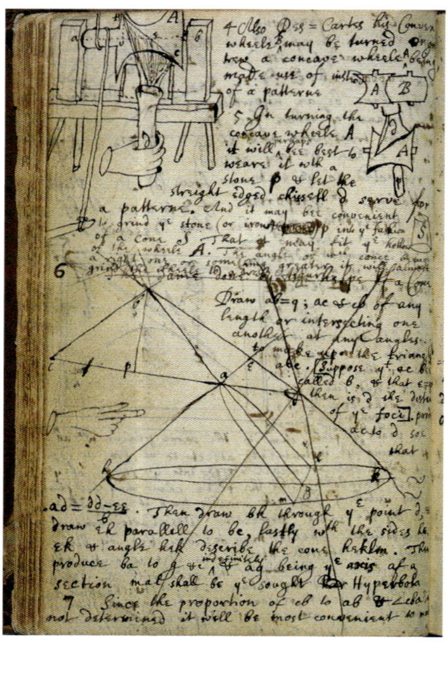

6

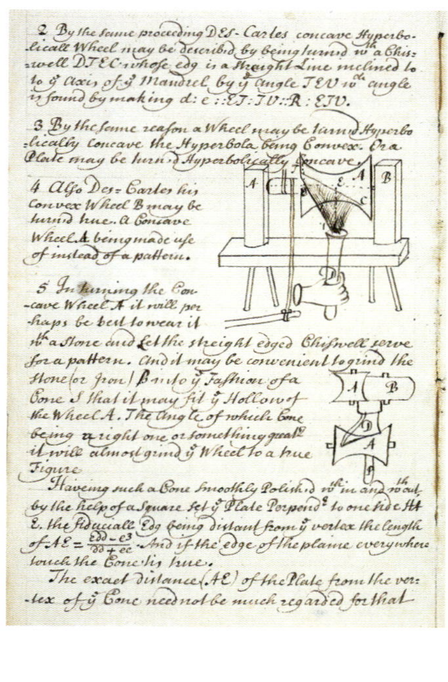

2 By the same proceeding Des-Cartes concave Hyperbolicall Wheel may be describ'd by being turn'd wth a Chiswell DTEC whose edg is a straight Line inclined to to ye Axis of ye Mandrel by ye angle TEV wch angle is found by making d : e :: ET : TV :: R : ETV.

3 By the same reason a Wheel may be turn'd Hyperbolically Concave the Hyperbola being Convex. Or a Plate may be turn'd Hyperbolically concave.

4 Also Des-Cartes his Convex Wheel B may be turn'd true. a Concave Wheel A being made use of instead of a pattern.

5 In turning the Concave Wheel A it will perhaps be best to wear it wth a Stone and let the streight edged Chiswell serve for a pattern. And it may be convenient to grind the Stone (or Iron) B into ye Fashion of a Cone S that it may fit ye Hollow of the Wheel A. The Angle of which Cone being a right one or something greatr it will almost grind ye Wheel to a true Figure.

Haveing such a Cone smoothly Polish'd wth in and wth out, by the help of a Square set ye Plate Perpendr to one side AE. the Fiduciall Edg being distant from ye vertex the length of $AE = \frac{edd - e^3}{dd + ee}$. And if the edge of the plaine everywhere touch the Cone 'tis true.

The exact distance (AE) of the Plate from the vertex of ye Cone need not be much regarded for that

7

Descartes' findings about refraction at curved surfaces. This is probably the date of the composition of the essay 'Of Refractions', part of which is displayed here. Newton later told Oldenburg that he had first applied himself to grinding lenses that were not spherical in the winter of 1666 and this essay includes the detailed description of a machine for shaping a wheel to a hyperbolical profile, which could later be used for grinding lenses. Such a machine had been discussed in chapter ten of *La dioptrique*, but Newton improved the design and gave a geometrical demonstration of its operation. The final two leaves from Newton's 'Of Refractions', which deal with compound lenses and the aberration of light refracted at a spherical surface, are missing from the notebook. They can now be found in the Macclesfield Collection, box 43.

Alan E. Shapiro (ed.), *The Optical Papers of Isaac Newton*, vol. 1 (Cambridge, 1984), 7–8; D.T. Whiteside (ed.), *The Mathematical Papers of Isaac Newton*, 8 vols (Cambridge, 1967–81), vol. 1, 47–88, 91–119, 219–33, 238–44, 298–321, 348–63, 559–76; A. Rupert Hall, 'Further Optical Experiments of Isaac Newton', *Annals of Science*, 11 (1955), 27–43.

Assessed 'Not fit to be printed' on behalf of Newton's executors by Thomas Pellet (25 September 1727); presented to Cambridge University Library by the fifth Earl of Portsmouth. See *A Catalogue of the Portsmouth Collection of Books and Papers written by or belonging to Sir Isaac Newton* (Cambridge, 1888), p. 48.

10 CAMBRIDGE UNIVERSITY LIBRARY, MACCLESFIELD COLLECTION, BOX 3/6

(figure 7)

19.2 × 12.7 cm

The presence of two stray leaves from one of Newton's notebooks among the papers in the Macclesfield Collection is not wholly surprising. The mathematician, William Jones (1675–1749), who was tutor to the children of Thomas Parker, later Earl of Macclesfield, had obtained many of the papers of John Collins (see catalogue number 38) in 1708, including a number of manuscripts and letters that Newton had sent to Collins. Jones sought to publish these, and, largely because of Newton's dispute with Leibniz over the invention of the calculus, was given permission to edit some of them. It is apparent from notebooks in the Macclesfield Collection that, at some point, Jones had wider access to other manuscripts that remained in Newton's possession. He seems have examined the notebook described above (catalogue number 9) since Newton had himself already decided that it bore witness to some of his earliest work on geometry and infinite series, leading up to the discovery of the calculus. Indeed, Newton had inserted an entry to that effect on 4 July 1699. Jones, however, had mathematical and philosophical interests that went beyond the quarrel over the calculus, and was generally curious about the history of Newton's work. In addition to the copies by Collins that he had now possessed, Jones therefore had several of Newton's own manuscripts copied into fresh notebooks, often bound in blue or grey pasteboard. In some cases, it is clear that manuscripts were damaged and leaves displaced when copies were made for Collins and later for Jones, for example from Newton's essay 'Of Refractions'.

'Of Refractions' was one of the essays of which Jones wanted to keep a copy. The handwriting of the transcription, which includes the contents of the leaves that were removed from the original notebook is not wholly dissimilar to that of Collins, but is more likely to be that of a copyist employed by Jones to transcribe mathematical and philosophical works. The transcription carries the title 'OPTICAL Papers of Sr Is. Newton' on its cover and is limited to the essay 'Of Refractions'. It is displayed here open to show Newton's design for a machine to shape a wheel to a hyperbolical profile.

Richard S. Westfall, *Never at Rest. A Biography of Isaac Newton* (Cambridge, 1980), p. 717; Cambridge University Library Ms. Add. 7339, f. 227 (letter from H.W. Turnbull, 17 July 1953).

Purchased from the Earl of Macclesfield by Cambridge University Library, August 2000.

11 CAMBRIDGE UNIVERSITY LIBRARY, MS. ADD. 3975, p. 15
(figures 8 and 9)
17.6 × 11.5 cm
Bound notebook of 174 leaves, paginated throughout.

Newton probably began making notes in this book in 1665 and 1666. The entries that he made then followed on both in subject matter and source material from some of the topics in his philosophical commonplace book (catalogue number 2). They fill the first twenty-two pages of this notebook, constituting an essay 'Of Colours' and are further broken down into 64 numbered sections or 'experiments' on pages 1 to 16. Newton's observations in these sections move from the appearance of colour given off by different bodies, through experiments with prisms in which he determines that blue and red light appear to be refracted differently, to investigations of the ability to perceive colour and of the anatomy of the eye. In experiments 58 and 59, Newton writes:

> I tooke a bodkine gh & put it betwixt my eye & [the] bone as neare to [the] backside of my eye as I could: & pressing my eye [with the] end of it (soe as to make [the] curvature a, bcdef in my eye) there appeared severall white darke & coloured circles r, s, t, &c. Which circles were plainest when I continued to rub my eye [with the] point of [the] bodkine, but if I held my eye & [the] bodkin still, though I continued to presse my eye [with] it yet [the] circles would grow faint & often disappeare untill I removed [them] by moving my eye or [the] bodkin.
>
> If [the] experiment were done in a light roome so [that] though my eyes were shut some light would get through their lidds There appeared a greate broade blewish darke circle outmost (as ts), & [within] that another light spot srs whose colour was much like [that] in [the] rest of [the] eye as at k. Within [which] spot appeared still another blew spot r espetially if I pressed my eye hard & [with] a small pointed bodkin. & outmost at vt appeared a verge of light.

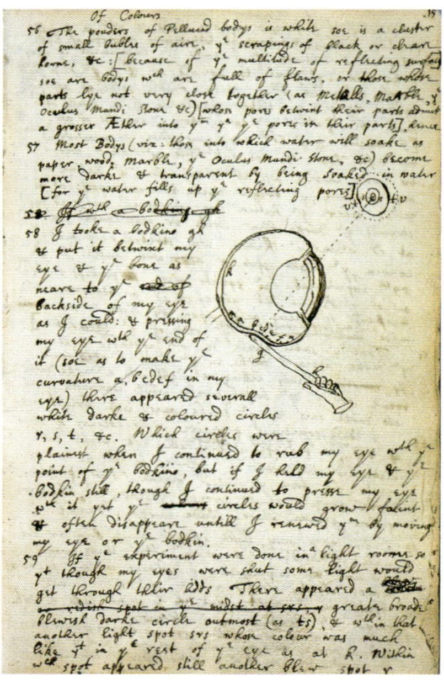

8

FIGURE 8
Newton's experiment with a bodkin, Ms. Add. 3975, p. 15.

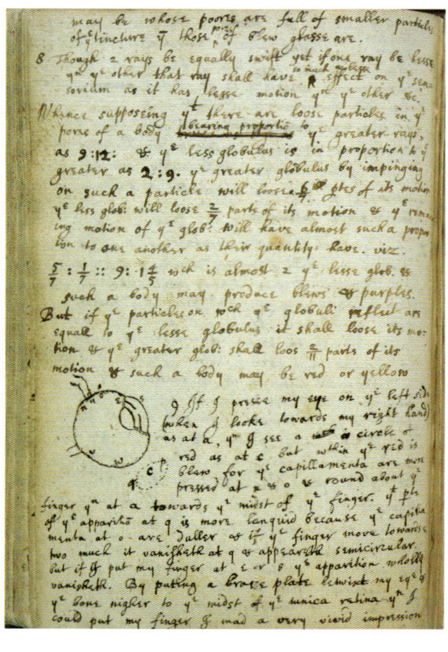

9

FIGURE 9
An experiment to put pressure on the eye, Ms. Add. 3996, f. 123v.

This account is illustrated with the diagram displayed here. Newton's interest in performing these experiments, however, was not confined to making optical or anatomical discoveries. As the entries in his earlier philosophical commonplace book indicate, Newton was also concerned with the way in which apparent sensations might in fact be the product of imagination and with the question of whether what one saw might be controlled by the nerves, and thus perhaps by the soul itself, rather than by some mechanical process of experience. These were issues that bothered both Descartes and Robert Boyle, on whose work on colour Newton was building, and some of the leading thinkers of contemporary Cambridge, in particular Henry More (1614–1687). More had also grown up in Grantham and had been one of the first English converts to Cartesianism before he became suspicious that Descartes' mechanical philosophy left too little role for the activities of spirits and the soul. Newton's experiments with his own eyes, as well as his investigation of the anatomy both of the human eye (which follows experiment 64 in this manuscript) and of a sheep's eye, need to be interpreted in this context.

One of the entries in Newton's philosophical commonplace book describes another experiment similar to that in the essay 'Of Colours', which is illustrated here as figure 9. Newton had been considering the question of whether the porosity of bodies may have some effect on the colours that they give off, perhaps by hindering the motion of rays of light. To investigate this, Newton experimented with the effects of putting pressure on his own eyeball:

> If I presse my eye on [the] left side (when I looke towards my right hand) as at a, [then] I see a circle of red as at c but [within the] red is blew for [the] capillamenta are more pressed at n & o & round about [the] finger [than] at a towards [the] midst of [the] finger. [That parte] of [the apparition] at q is more languid because [the] capillamenta at o are duller & if [the] finger move towards e two much it vanisheth at q & appeareth semicircular. but if I put my finger at e or s [the] apparition wholly vanisheth. By putting a brasse plate betwixt my eye & [the] bone nigher to [the] midst of [the] tunica retina [than] I could put my finger I [made] a very vivid impression. But of an ellipticall figure because [the] edge of [the] plate [with which] I prest my eye was long & not round like my finger

Newton also described an experiment involving looking at the sun and then at a piece of white paper. He claimed that he could replicate what he saw subsequently by imagining that he had looked at the sun 'whence I gather that my fantasy and the Sun had the same operation upon the spirits in my optic nerve'.

Although these investigations perhaps seem hazardous to us, Newton was far from being the only one of his contemporaries to regard his own body as a suitable object for experiment. His reports of his experiences retain throughout a detachment which appears clinical, yet in fact these were potentially some of the most moving as well as the most painful experiments that the young Newton could have performed. This was because the demonstration of how active spirits or the soul might affect perception could also be a powerful weapon against materialism and its bed-fellow, atheism.

After writing his essay 'Of Colours' and then making notes from various works of Robert Boyle, particularly *New Experiments and Observations touching Cold* (1665) and *The Origine of Formes and Qualities* (1666), Newton may have abandoned this notebook for a year or two. However, the interest in the shaping and ordering of matter that is apparent both in the notes that Newton took from Boyle and in his own experiments on colours, resurfaced shortly afterwards in entries based on fresh reading in the literature of alchemy. Initially, many of these were also drawn from Boyle, including some references to the work of Joan Baptista van Helmont, but they soon contained evidence of Newton's assimilation of the writings of the mid-seventeenth-century alchemist, George Starkey (also known as Eirenaeus Philalethes). Although many of Newton's notes were simply references to his reading, it is often clear that he was also recording his own attempts to reproduce the experiments that he was studying. This is especially apparent in the dated entries from the early and mid-1680s, by which time Newton's library contained copies of all the works by Starkey to which he refers in this manuscript, but it is also suggested by notes that may have been made as early as 1669.

J.E. McGuire and Martin Tamny (eds), *Certain Philosophical Questions: Newton's Trinity Notebook* (Cambridge, 1983), especially pp. 216–325, 394–6, 430–47, 466–89; A. Rupert Hall, 'Further Optical Experiments of Isaac Newton', *Annals of Science*, 11 (1955), 27–43; Rob Iliffe, '"That puzleing Problem": Isaac Newton and the Political Physiology of Self', *Medical History*, 39 (1995), 433–58; Cambridge University Library, Ms. Add. 3970, f. 650; Betty Jo Teeter Dobbs, *The Foundations of Newton's Alchemy* (Cambridge, 1975), pp. 126–93; William R. Newman, *Gehennical*

Fire. The Lives of George Starkey, an American Alchemist in the Scientific Revolution (Cambridge, Mass., 1994), pp. 228–43.

Assessed 'Not fit to be printed' on behalf of Newton's executors by Thomas Pellet (25 September 1727); presented to Cambridge University Library by the fifth Earl of Portsmouth. See *A Catalogue of the Portsmouth Collection of Books and Papers written by or belonging to Sir Isaac Newton* (Cambridge, 1888), pp. 21–4.

12 THOMAS SPRAT, *The History of the Royal-Society of London, for the Improving of Natural Knowledge*

(London, 1667)
(figure 10)
4°: A–B^4, A–3I^4
17.3 × 12 cm
Trinity College Library, Cambridge, NQ 9/28

According to the accounts given in one of his early notebooks (catalogue number 3), Newton purchased this book for 7s. shortly after it was published in 1667. He had just performed the Act for his Bachelor's degree and may not yet have been elected to the minor fellowship of Trinity that he held from October. As early as 1663, the Royal Society, which was founded in 1660, had begun to consider publishing a *History*, in order to present some sense of its intentions to a broader public. Thomas Sprat (1635–1715), a protégé of one of the most powerful and active fellows of the early Royal Society, John Wilkins, was chosen to write the work. Wilkins was closely involved in its composition, which was however interrupted in 1665 and 1666 as a consequence of the disruption caused by the plague and the Great Fire. Other fellows of the

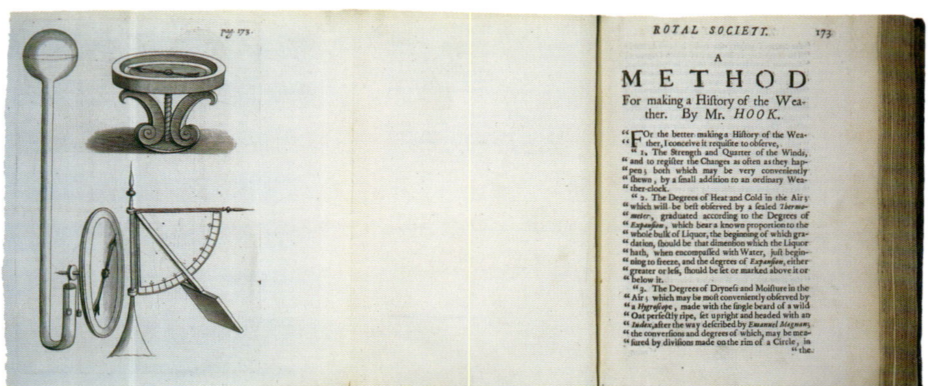

FIGURE 10
Thomas Sprat, *History of the Royal Society* (1667), folding plate of meteorological instruments, Trinity College, NQ 9/28, facing p. 173.

Society, notably its secretary Henry Oldenburg, also contributed to the *History*, which included accounts of their work and of projects that the Society wished, at least in theory, to promote. For example, one of several contributions by Robert Hooke was 'A Method for making a History of the Weather', which included designs for meteorological instruments that were illustrated on an accompanying plate. When it did appear, Sprat's *History* was not an unqualified success. Indeed, in the controversies over the new science that blew up in the late 1660s, it seems to have provided much ammunition for critics of the Royal Society.

John Harrison, *The Library of Isaac Newton* (Cambridge, 1978), p. 242; Thomas Sprat, *The History of the Royal Society of London*, ed. J.I. Cope and H.W. Jones (London, 1959); Paul Wood, 'Methodology and Apologetics: Thomas Sprat's *History of the Royal Society*', *British Journal for the History of Science*, 13 (1980), 1–26; Michael Hunter, *Establishing the New Science* (Woodbridge, 1989), pp. 45–71.

Listed by the booksellers who appraised Newton's library for his executors; bought with the rest of the library by John Huggins in 1727. Bookplate of Charles Huggins. Bookplate of James Musgrave, with shelfmark F5–17. Presented to Trinity College, Cambridge, on 30 October 1943 by the Pilgrim Trust.

13 CAMBRIDGE UNIVERSITY LIBRARY, MS. ADD. 3958, f. 5r

(figure 11)

19.6 × 15 cm

In the mid-1660s, Newton seems to have begun taking notes from books on separate sheets of paper as well as in pocket-books. His usual method was to fold a single, full sheet of paper in four, creating a booklet of four leaves or eight pages. He would normally cut the edge between pages two and three but leave that between pages six and seven uncut, even if he had written on those pages. The first notes according to this manner that Newton took appear to have been from Robert Hooke's *Micrographia* (1665). Newton was interested in Hooke's comments on the material structure of various substances as well as in his ideas about the nature of light and colours. Newton's acquaintance with Descartes' optical thought and his own experiences made him confident enough to express a rare note of criticism concerning some of Hooke's explanations of colour, for example in his description of Muscovy glass. It was more usual, however, for Newton's notes to be straightforward records of those parts of books that had interested him, as in the case of Sprat's *History*.

The longest note that Newton made on his reading of Sprat concerned the reports of unusual phenomena in nature and of strange

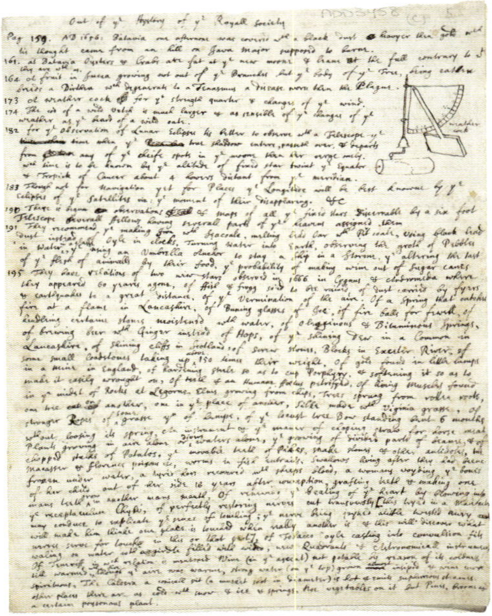
Out of yᵉ History of yᵉ Royall Society

FIGURE 11
Newton's notes taken from his reading of Sprat's *History of the Royal Society* (1667), Ms. Add. 3958, f. 5r.

devices that the Royal Society had received. He also recorded additional information about Hooke's ideas of matter and noted methods of making telescopic observations. He was certainly interested in summarising the range of activities practised by the early fellows of the Society. The most striking aspect of this sheet of notes, however, is the copy that Newton made of a design for a weather-cock from the folding plate that illustrated Hooke's 'Method for making a History of the Weather'.

Newton was sufficiently impressed by the activities of the early Royal Society, and by the intriguing reports that its members collected, to take notes from the journal produced by the Society's secretary, Henry Oldenburg. He entered these in a further booklet of notes, headed 'Out of Philosophicall Transactions', which covered numbers one to twenty-four (1665–7) of the journal.

A. Rupert Hall and Marie Boas Hall (eds), *Unpublished Scientific Papers of Isaac Newton* (Cambridge, 1962), pp. 397–413; Cambridge University Library, Ms. Add. 3958, ff. 1–4, 9–24.

Presented to Cambridge University Library by the fifth Earl of Portsmouth. See *A Catalogue of the Portsmouth Collection of Books and Papers written by or belonging to Sir Isaac Newton* (Cambridge, 1888), p. 1.

14 CAMBRIDGE UNIVERSITY LIBRARY, MS. ADD. 3973, f. 25a
20.4 × 16 cm

In his alchemical work, Newton often used the same method of taking notes in a booklet constructed from a single folded sheet. This manuscript consists of several of these booklets, the earliest of which is dated December 1678 and the latest February 1696. As the practice of dating them suggests, Newton's notes relate to specific chemical experiments and appear to record laboratory activity, often referring to operations that had been performed at an earlier time or using substances that had already been prepared. Records of some of these experiments were also entered in the alchemical notebook that Newton was keeping (catalogue number 11), sometimes in a more complete form. Newton also kept a note there of his purchases of chemicals in London during 1687, from 'Mr Stonestreet Druggest by Bow Church', and in 1693 from Timothy Langley, who had succeeded Stonestreet in the business. Much of the experimental work that Newton chronicled was carried out in the early 1680s, when Newton was living in E3, Great Court, to the right of the Great Gate into Trinity College (see figure 31). Newton seems to have had a separate laboratory constructed for him by this time. His amanuensis, Humphrey Newton, observed his master's chemical activities, which were particularly extensive in spring and autumn, 'at [which] Times he used to imploy about 6 weeks in his Elaboratory, the Fire scarcely going out either Night or Day, he siting up one Night, as I did another, till he had finished his Chymical Experiments, in [the] Performances of [which] he was [the] most accurate, strict, exact'.

Many of Newton's experiments at this time concern chemical transformations of sal ammoniac (NH_4Cl, or ammonium chloride), processes that were derived largely from his reading of the publications of George Starkey. Like Starkey, Newton was careful to record the weight of chemical substances that he produced. From this, and from Newton's interest in experiments leading to sublimation, it seems possible to conclude that he was searching for the alchahest, a substance that could reduce matter to its essential components, about which van Helmont had written extensively. In addition to these authors, Newton's notes on his experiments at this time also show the influence of works attributed to Basilius Valentinus, which Newton started to read alongside the writings of the German alchemist Michael Maier (see catalogue number 52) in about 1670.

Other experimental notes by Newton in this manuscript, including those on display, date from a later period of intense alchemical investigation in the early 1690s. This activity continued at least until Newton's departure for London in spring 1696. It was encouraged by a new acquaintance of Newton, for a time his closest friend, the Swiss mathematician Nicolas Fatio de Duillier. Fatio helped Newton to acquire and read alchemical texts, in particular those in French, and encouraged him both to revise the *Principia* and to develop ideas about the cause of gravity. Newton and Fatio were both interested in the process of fermentation, through which metals could be made ready for transmutation. They corresponded about the methods involved during 1693 and, between December 1692 and June 1693, Newton took notes on a series of relevant experiments that he was carrying out. These notes were theoretical as well as practical and surely drew on Newton's wide alchemical reading. That reading would also have alerted Newton to the analogy between chemical reactions involving the compounds of metals and the processes of distillation by which beer and spirits are manufactured. Newton's notes opened in December 1692 with an account of the production and virtue of barm (the froth on fermenting malt liquor, which can itself be used in fermentation) in brewing. One of the publications of William Yworth, a chemist from Rotterdam who had recently settled in London, contained a similar description of brewing. Newton owned a copy of this book, *Introitus apertus ad artem distillationis; or the Whole Art of Distillation* (London, 1692), although it seems likely that he came by it a few years later, by which time he was acting as Yworth's patron.

The illnesses that both Fatio and Newton suffered during the early 1690s may have provided an additional reason for intensive chemical activity. After all, one of the aims of alchemical transmutation was to produce a healing elixir. It is more likely, however, that Newton's investigations were linked to attempts to understand the nature of matter and force that built on his earlier experimental work and increasingly preoccupied him after the publication of the *Principia*. Nevertheless, Newton's alchemical activity at this time may have had implications for his health. His notes reveal that he must have exposed himself to high levels of antimony, as well as to lead, iron, copper, mercury, and their compounds, during the experiments that he conducted in 1693. Throughout the year, Newton displayed symptoms of illness, and his correspondence from the autumn suggests that he suffered a serious collapse in his self-confidence and ability to trust others, if not a genuine mental breakdown. Although it is possible that metal poisoning contributed to Newton's suffering, it is just as probable that his long-standing anxiety about publicity and problems created by the closeness of his relationship to Fatio generated the sickness and unease that he experienced.

Marie Boas and Rupert Hall, 'Newton's Chemical Experiments', *Archives internationales d'histoire des sciences*, 11 (1958), 113–52; Richard S. Westfall, *Never at Rest. A Biography of Isaac Newton* (Cambridge, 1980), pp. 290–310, 359–69, 527–39; King's College, Cambridge, Keynes Ms. 135; Lord Adrian, 'Newton's Rooms in Trinity', *Notes and Records of the Royal Society of London*, 17 (1962), 17–24; Betty Jo Teeter Dobbs, *The Janus Faces of Genius* (Cambridge, 1991), pp. 170–4, 288–92 (printing Ms. Add. 3973, ff. 25a–28b, although with frequent mistakes in transcription); Karin Figala, 'Newton, Isaac', in Claus Priesner and Karin Figala (eds), *Alchemie: Lexikon einer hermetischen Wissenschaft* (Munich, 1998), pp. 252–8; William R. Newman, *Gehennical Fire. The Lives of George Starkey, an American Alchemist in the Scientific Revolution* (Cambridge, Mass., 1994), pp. 175–88; H. W. Turnbull, J.F. Scott, A.R. Hall and Laura Tilling (eds), *The Correspondence of Isaac Newton*, 7 vols (Cambridge, 1959–77), vol. 3, 260–3, 265–70; L.W. Johnson and M.L. Wolbarsht, 'Mercury Poisioning: A Probable Cause of Isaac Newton's Physical and Mental Ills', *Notes and Records of the Royal Society of London*, 34 (1979–80), 1–9; P.E. Spargo and C.A. Pounds, 'Newton's "Derangement of the Intellect". New Light on an Old Problem', *Notes and Records of the Royal Society of London*, 34 (1979–80), 11–32; R.W. Ditchburn, 'Newton's Illness of 1692–3', *Notes and Records of the Royal Society of London*, 35 (1980), 1–16.

Presented to Cambridge University Library by the fifth Earl of Portsmouth. See *A Catalogue of the Portsmouth Collection of Books and Papers written by or belonging to Sir Isaac Newton* (Cambridge, 1888), pp. 19–20.

15 GERARDUS JOANNES VOSSIUS, *De theologia gentili, et physiologia Christiana; sive de origine ac progressu idololatriae*
(Amsterdam, 1641)
(figure 12)
4°: π^{2}, A-2P^{4}, $\star$-4$\star^{4}$, 5$\star^{2}$, 2Q-4X^{4}, 4Y^{6}, +-5+^{4}
17.3 × 13cm
Trinity College, Cambridge, NQ 8/46

During the 1680s, Newton deepened his interest in the thought and belief of the ancient world. He developed the notion that he might be a representative of a remnant of individuals who preserved or were able to recover knowledge of the true religion and the true natural philosophy. This idea manifested itself in a number of ways. It may lie behind some of Newton's alchemical reading and experiment. Many alchemical authors claimed to have had access to ancient and secret wisdom and some also suggested that they belonged to a hidden brotherhood dedicated to passing on such knowledge. By the 1690s, Newton's interest in ancient philosophy had certainly begun to be expressed in his own natural philosophy (see catalogue number 56). Yet, it was most apparent in his theological writing, which took a new turn during the mid-1680s and early 1690s.

In these years, Newton expanded his concern with the corruption of the Christian religion through the growth of idolatry into a reconstruction of the origins of human religion. He argued for the continuity of essential points of doctrine between a primitive religion, which had degenerated into paganism; Judaism, which had been corrupted after the time of the prophets; and Christianity, which had been led into idolatry by proponents of the doctrine of the Trinity.

These developments in Newton's ideas were prompted in part by the widening range of his reading. The volume on display here contains two works, published together, both of which Newton used extensively. One of these is an edition of Maimonides on idolatry by Dionysius Vossius (1641). The other is a book by Dionysius Vossius' father, Gerardus Joannes, which dealt with the history of idolatry through a wide-ranging examination of pagan, Jewish, and Christian sources. The writings of the Vossius family provide good examples of the books that came to make up the bulk of Newton's library. These were works of erudition, normally published in Newton's lifetime and predominantly written in English or Latin. They were often editions or compilations that based themselves on much earlier writings but were usually themselves the product of humanist techniques of scholarship. Although there is evidence that Newton read many of these books from cover to cover, he also used many of them much more selectively. In particular, it was his habit to mark passages that interested him by turning down page corners so that they pointed to the exact phrase that he wished to recall. These phrases were often themselves references or quotations from other works, perhaps accompanied by translations by the author that Newton was himself reading. Newton would later incorporate the information that he had gathered in this way from his reading into his own theological and historical writing, thus furnishing it with a seemingly inexhaustible range of quotations and source material.

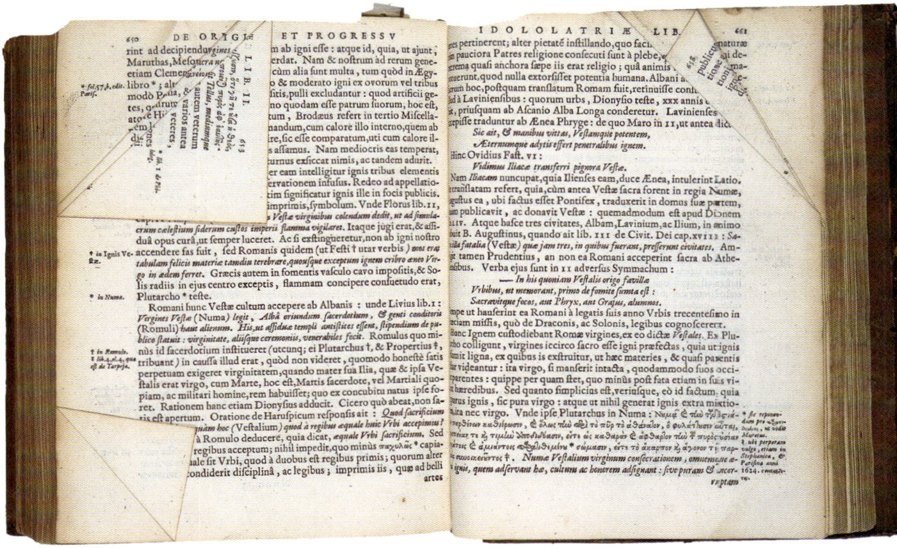

FIGURE 12
Vossius' *De theologia gentili, et physiologia Christiana*, from Newton's library and showing his habit of turning down the corners of pages to mark passages of interest or for quotation, Trinity College, Cambridge, NQ 8/46, pp. 654–5.

Gerardus Joannes Vossius (1577–1649) was one of the most prominent scholars of the early seventeenth century. He held a chair of Eloquence and Chronology at Leiden University from 1622, later becoming Professor of Greek as well. In 1632, he delivered the oration that opened the Athenaeum Illustre (the predecessor of the University of Amsterdam), where he was one of two founding professors. He was the author of standard works for the study of Greek and of rhetoric (see catalogue number 2). *De theologia gentili* was the crowning achievement of Vossius' historical writing. It examined a huge range of sources to give an account of the development of polytheistic beliefs in classical, teutonic, oriental, and even American history and mythology. Newton used this book extensively as a source for his own essay, 'Theologiae gentilis origines philosophicae' ('The Philosophical Origins of Gentile Theology'), whose title was even derived from Vossius. Written in the mid-1680s, this work described the form of worship practised by the adherents of the true, primitive religion. It suggested that they had prayed and sacrificed at sacred places where perpetual fires burned. This kind of religious practice had survived in the Temple at Jerusalem and, to some extent, in pagan temples, especially those of the cult of Vesta. Much of the information for Newton's argument could be found in *De theologia gentili*. For example, in the pages on display (pp. 654–5) Vossius quoted several classical authors who had written about the Vestal cult and the establishment of its temple at Rome by Numa Pompilius, the mythical successor of Romulus. These are the passages that Newton marked by turning down the corners of pages 654 and 655, and references to them appear both in his theological writings of the late 1680s and early 1690s and in much later works of chronology and natural philosophy.

Richard S. Westfall, 'Isaac Newton's *Theologiae Gentilis Origines Philosophicae*', in W. Warren Wagar (ed.), *The Secular Mind* (New York, 1982), pp. 15–34; Jewish National and University Library, Jerusalem, Mss. Yahuda 16, 17, 41; John Harrison, *The Library of Isaac Newton* (Cambridge, 1978), pp. 1–27, 58–78, 258; Richard H. Popkin, 'Polytheism, Deism, and Newton', in James E. Force and Richard H. Popkin, *Essays on the Context, Nature, and Influence of Isaac Newton's Theology* (Dordrecht, 1990), pp. 27–42; C.S.M. Rademaker, SS.CC., *Life and Work of Gerardus Joannes Vossius (1577–1649)* (Assen, 1981), pp. 306–10; Nicholas Wickenden, *G.J. Vossius and the Humanist Concept of History* (Assen, 1993), pp. 27–30, 142–51.

Listed by the booksellers who appraised Newton's library for his executors; bought with the rest of the library by John Huggins in 1727. Bookplate of Charles Huggins. Bookplate of James Musgrave, with shelfmark C1–12. Presented to Trinity College, Cambridge, on 30 October 1943 by the Pilgrim Trust.

16 CAMBRIDGE UNIVERSITY LIBRARY, MS. Dd. 9.46, f. 1r

32.6 × 21 cm

110 folio leaves in a modern binding

This manuscript, headed 'De motu Corporum Liber primus', is again in the hand of Humphrey Newton, although the text has been extensively corrected by Newton himself. It was deposited as the lectures given by the Lucasian Professor in 1684 and 1685, and was labelled by Newton to give the appearance that it consisted of nineteen lectures, delivered in two series, beginning in October 1684 and October 1685 respectively. Although Newton had indeed deposited copies of earlier lectures, delivered between 1670 and 1683, it seems most unlikely that he ever delivered this text orally. Rather, it formed a draft for what would become Book I of the *Principia*. The text is broken into two sequences, both incomplete. The first of these contains material relating to the laws of motion and the definitions in Book I; the second, which runs from the corollary to proposition XVI to proposition LIV, is much closer to the final manuscript of the *Principia* and includes reworked material from the preceding sequence of pages. Additional material from this draft of the *Principia* may be found in Ms. Add. 3965.3, ff. 7–14; further pages of revisions may also be found elsewhere in the Portsmouth Collection.

Newton probably composed this manuscript between spring and autumn 1685. It was the successor to an earlier treatise ('De motu') that Newton had prepared in the months before November 1684, and greatly expanded its treatment of celestial dynamics. Like its predecessor, 'De motu Corporum Liber primus' was formulated in terms of classical geometry but depended on an understanding of force and motion that derived in part from Newton's own discovery of infinitesimals. It presented Newton's three laws of motion for the first time in the form that they would take in the finished text of the *Principia*.

In addition to its mathematical importance, the manuscript is of interest because of the light that it sheds on Newton's working habits in the mid-1680s. The first page of the text, which is on display, provides a good example. Expanding on his work in 'De motu', Newton composed a series of definitions of matter, motion, and force (Ms. Add. 3965.5, f. 21r) as an introduction to his treatment of the laws of motion. A revised version of this text was then copied by Humphrey Newton, perhaps from dictation by Newton. Newton's amanuensis confined himself to the recto side of each folio, leaving the verso blank for Newton's own alterations and additions. Humphrey Newton's text was generally fluent and carefully written, nevertheless Newton's corrections to it were often brutal. This is especially clear at the start of the manuscript, where Newton has extensively rewritten the 'definitiones', inserting a number of passages that reflect his growing sense of the need for perfect clarity. Some of these alterations (for example, in what became definition 3, 'Materiae vis insita') produced the exact wording that Newton preserved when he had Humphrey Newton write out the manuscript of the printer's copy of the *Principia*. Other changes, for example the cancellation of the original definitions 2 and 3, and the renumbering of the subsequent definitions, represented a partial return by Newton to the form of his earlier draft. Although there is evidence that Newton considered a further expansion of these definitions, in general the corrections that he made in this manuscript established the shape that they would take in the finished text of the *Principia*.

D.T. Whiteside (ed.), *The Preliminary Manuscripts for Isaac Newton's 1687 Principia, 1684–1686* (Cambridge, 1989), pp. xvi–xvii, 37–238 (pp. 37–215 print a facsimile of this manuscript; the folio on display may be found at p. 37); I. Bernard Cohen,

Introduction to Newton's 'Principia' (Cambridge, 1971), pp. 82–98; D.T. Whiteside (ed.), *The Mathematical Papers of Isaac Newton*, 8 vols (Cambridge, 1967–81), vol. 6, especially pp. 92–187; A. Rupert Hall and Marie Boas Hall (eds), *Unpublished Scientific Papers of Isaac Newton* (Cambridge, 1962), pp. 237–92; John Herivel, *The Background to Newton's Principia* (Oxford, 1965), pp. 98–102, 321–6; J. Edleston (ed.), *Correspondence of Sir Isaac Newton and Professor Cotes* (London, 1850), pp. xci-vii; Richard S. Westfall, *Force in Newton's Physics* (London, 1971), pp. 424–525; François de Gandt, *Force and Geometry in Newton's Principia* (Princeton, 1995). Exhibited in 1987: 'The Making of Newton's "Principia" (1664–1687)', case 5, item 1.

17 CAMBRIDGE UNIVERSITY ARCHIVES, O.III.8/2

(figure 13)

8.2 × 13.5 cm and 7.7 × 15.1 cm

Josephus Beaumont eligit Mrum Isaacum Newton, hujus Academiae Delegatum ad Ordinum Conventu Westmonasterii propediem habendum.

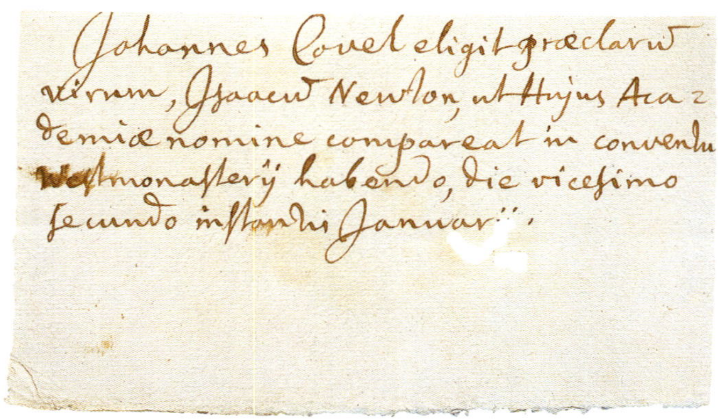
Johannes Covel eligit praeclarum virum, Isaacum Newton, ut Hujus Aca-demiae nomine compareat in conventu Westmonasterij habendo, die vicesimo secundo instantis Januarii.

FIGURE 13
Two of the ballots cast for Newton to serve as MP for Cambridge University at the Convention Parliament, 15 January 1689, University Archives, O.III.8/2.

These two scraps of paper are two of the ballots that were cast for Newton to serve as Member of Parliament for Cambridge University at the Convention Parliament. The election took place on 15 January 1689. The Universities of Oxford and Cambridge had each won the right to send two burgesses to the House of Commons in 1604. Since then, there had been elections for every new Parliament. The Vice-Chancellors of each university usually tried to control these events and the franchise seems to have been limited to senior members who were of the standing of Master of Arts. By the later seventeenth century, it was usual at Cambridge for the vote to be by ballot, although the name of the elector had to be written on the ballot paper as well as the name of the preferred candidate. The Convention was summoned on 29 December 1688, after the landing in England of William of Orange and his successful march on London. It was responsible for the creation of an acceptable constitutional settlement that took into account the flight of James II and the revolutionary events of summer and autumn 1688.

The election in 1689 was a close contest. There were three candidates: Edward Finch of Christ's College, who was brother to one of the candidates in the Oxford University election and to the Earl of Nottingham, one of the peers who had so far supported William of Orange; Sir Robert Sawyer, who may have had the support of the Archbishop of Canterbury, at that stage a prominent critic of James II; and Newton. Despite anxiety about his status as a non-resident member of the University, Sawyer received 125 votes and was elected alongside Newton, for whom 122 votes were cast. 117 electors backed the disappointed Finch.

Newton's success in this contest owed much to the reputation he had forged over the previous two years, when he had helped to lead opposition to James II's attempts to force the University to admit Alban Francis. Francis was a Benedictine monk and it was proposed in February 1687 that he should not have to take the customary oath of allegiance to the Church of England. Newton was one of the ringleaders of resistance to this suggestion and proved a determined (not to say intolerant) defender of the University's privileges from the interference of the king and his allies. Given his own heterodoxy, Newton's concern was perhaps more with the subversion of a Catholic plot than the defence of the Church of England. Nevertheless he was instrumental in constructing the University's case and was one of those chosen to defend it before Judge Jeffreys at the Court of Ecclesiastical Commission. Although the Crown abandoned Father Francis, it was fortunate for Newton that external events altered so quickly in his favour. Once elected as an MP, Newton was a steadfast proponent of the regime created by the Revolution, and, despite his religious scruples, found nothing worthy of objection in oaths of loyalty to the new monarchs, William and Mary. The apparent purity of his ideological credentials also spared him the embarrassing investigations and censure that awaited his fellow burgess, Sawyer.

The two ballots on display were cast by Joseph Beaumont and John Covel. Beaumont (1616–99), Master of Peterhouse and Regius Professor of Divinity, was a powerful defender of the privileges of the Church of England and a stickler for the traditions of the University. He had been one of the most outspoken critics of Henry More and of the Cambridge Platonists. It seems unlikely that he would have given his support to Newton, who had been a friend of More, without the events of 1687–8. Covel (1638–1722), by contrast, was the newly appointed Master of Christ's College and the University's Vice-Chancellor. Between 1681 and 1685 he had been chaplain to the Princess of Orange, who was now about to be proclaimed queen. Covel subsequently relied heavily on Newton's advice from Westminster during 1689, especially on the issue of taking the new oaths.

Newton did not stand for re-election to Parliament in 1690, but was persuaded by his Whig patrons to be a candidate in 1701, when he was again elected for the University. At the election in 1702, he stood down but he was a candidate in 1705, and was knighted by Queen Anne in Trinity College during the run-up to that election. This time, however, Newton received the fewest votes in a field of four candidates. He was humiliated in a bitterly fought party political contest in which knowledge of his friendships and religious leanings, if not of his covert heretical beliefs, may well have contributed to his failure. The mob was said to have cried 'No Fanatic, No Occasional Conformity' against the unsuccessful candidates during the election.

Millicent Barton Rex, *University Representation in England, 1604–1690* (London, 1954), pp. 300–20; Richard S. Westfall, *Never at Rest. A Biography of Isaac Newton* (Cambridge, 1980), pp. 623–6; H. W. Turnbull, J.F. Scott, A.R. Hall and Laura Tilling (eds), *The Correspondence of Isaac Newton*, 7 vols (Cambridge, 1959–77), vol. 2, 467–9; vol. 3, 1–3, 7–8, 10–24.

18 CAMBRIDGE UNIVERSITY LIBRARY, MS. ADD. 3966, f. 117r
30 × 18.6 cm

As a result of his political activity and exposure to the world of Westminster, Newton was able to explore the possibility of holding public office. He approached a number of friends during the early 1690s with this in mind. He also allowed himself to be consulted on issues of public policy, especially those in which a knowledge of mathematics played a role (see catalogue number 8). Newton's opportunities increased following the appointment of Charles Montague, who had been a fellow of Trinity, as Chancellor of the Exchequer. Newton's opinion had already been sought in connection with plans for recoinage. On 19 March 1696, Montague invited him to become Warden of the Mint. He perhaps intended this as a sinecure, from which Newton might draw an income of £500 a year. But Newton proved a dedicated public servant. He moved to London and oversaw much of the business associated with calling in old money and issuing new coin. He was zealous in the fight against counterfeiters and helped to plan the establishment of new Mints in regional centres. Following the death of Thomas Neale, Newton was appointed Master of the Mint on 26 December 1699, and was thus relieved of his resentment at having to serve in a subordinate post. Despite the need to provide securities, Newton's new office enabled him to become a rich man through the commission that he received on every pound of gold or silver minted, in addition to his salary of £500. It also made it possible for him to reward relatives, friends, and sympathisers with lucrative jobs. Newton was an active and successful Master, who reintroduced strict measures in coining and presided over several new ventures, generally attempting to raise the standard not only of gold and silver money but also of copper coin.

The letter on display is typical of many documents from Newton's time at the Mint. Although he was now wealthy, Newton's habit of saving scraps of paper for his own use did not die just because more and more business passed over his desk. Almost immediately after his nomination as Master of the Mint, Newton received this letter from Robert Blackborne at East India House, dated 30 December 1699. Its business related to an issue with which Newton had been familiar as Warden, the control of the machinery for minting coin. Blackborne was responding to a query from Newton about the right of the East India Company to request mills and presses from the Mint. Newton, however, preserved the paper generated by this routine matter and drew on it a few months later when he was engaged in calculations for his theory of the moon's motion. He covered Blackborne's original letter with calculations of the relative positions of the sun and the moon. These included estimates of the position of the sun and the moon at Greenwich on 1 January 1701 and may have related to a memorandum about the reform of the calendar that Newton prepared for the Royal Society in April 1700. Yet Newton's interest in calculating positions of the moon also played a larger role in his work at this time.

By February 1700, Newton had shared his ideas about the motion of the moon with his friend and client, the Scottish mathematician and Professor of Astronomy at Oxford, David Gregory. Gregory published Newton's lunar theory in Latin in 1702, and an English translation appeared in the same year. It represented an unsuccessful attempt to expand on the findings of the first edition of the *Principia*, in particular through the consideration of how three gravitating bodies (the sun, the earth, and the moon) act upon one another in a single system. It also promised to yield useful information for navigation at sea. Newton, however, found it impossible to derive the inequalities of the moon's motion from his theory of gravity, although he did set out the range of observations necessary to make accurate calculations. He incorporated a number of corrections to the account of the moon in the *Principia* (see catalogue number 43) as a new scholium to proposition xxxv of Book III of the second edition (1713) and continued to revise this part of the work in the third edition (1726).

Like so much of Newton's work on celestial dynamics, his theory of the moon's motion depended on access to accurate astronomical observations taken over a long period of time. In addition to historical series, especially those of the late sixteenth-century Danish astronomer Tycho Brahe, Newton based himself on information provided by his own observations and those of his contemporaries. The Astronomer Royal, John Flamsteed, was by far the most reliable source of this material, derived from his observations at Greenwich. Under strict conditions of secrecy, Flamsteed agreed to feed Newton with observations of the moon from 1694, but the two men had begun to quarrel by the beginning of 1699. Newton was subsequently able to use the political influence at his disposal to try to force Flamsteed to provide him with information. In particular, he was instrumental in the establishment of a

Committee of Referees to oversee the publication of Flamsteed's long-delayed star catalogue. But political change and delays at the press, allied to Falmsteed's intransigence, obstructed Newton's plans. By 1714, Flamsteed was at last able to break free of the controls that Newton had imposed.

Sir John Craig, *Newton at the Mint* (Cambridge, 1946); Richard S. Westfall, *Never at Rest. A Biography of Isaac Newton* (Cambridge, 1980), pp. 551–626; H. W. Turnbull, J.F. Scott, A.R. Hall and Laura Tilling (eds), *The Correspondence of Isaac Newton*, 7 vols (Cambridge, 1959–77), vol. 4, 195, 317–8 (printing this letter), 322–48; I. Bernard Cohen (ed.), *Isaac Newton's Theory of the Moon's Motion (1702)* (London, 1975); Francis Baily (ed.), *An Account of the Revd. John Flamsteed* (London, 1835).

Presented to Cambridge University Library by the fifth Earl of Portsmouth. See *A Catalogue of the Portsmouth Collection of Books and Papers written by or belonging to Sir Isaac Newton* (Cambridge, 1888), pp. 5–6.

19 CAMBRIDGE UNIVERSITY LIBRARY, MS. ADD. 3966, f. 232r
30.6 cm × 20 cm

This page comes from one of a number of tables of eclipses of the sun and the moon that Newton prepared, using data derived largely from the observations of Tycho Brahe and John Flamsteed. It helps to demonstrate the dependence of Newton's work on the history of astronomical observation as well as on the work of his contemporaries. Although it is hard to be certain of its date, it may well have been compiled in the mid-1690s, when Newton and Falmsteed corresponded extensively about lunar eclipses. At that time, Newton was also collecting the data for his theory of the moon's motion.

H. W. Turnbull, J.F. Scott, A.R. Hall and Laura Tilling (eds), *The Correspondence of Isaac Newton*, 7 vols (Cambridge, 1959–77), vol. 4, 73–114.

Presented to Cambridge University Library by the fifth Earl of Portsmouth. See *A Catalogue of the Portsmouth Collection of Books and Papers written by or belonging to Sir Isaac Newton* (Cambridge, 1888), pp. 5–6.

[Dating supported by the watermark (posthorn + HG/MC)]

about three foot radius (suppose a broad Object-glass of a three foot Telescope,) at the distance of about four or five foot from thence, through which all those colours may at once be transmitted, and made by its Refraction to convene at a further distance of about ten or twelve feet. If at that distance you intercept this light with a sheet of white paper, you will see the colours converted into whiteness again by being mingled. But it is requisite, that the *Prisme* and *Lens* be placed steddy, and that the paper, on which the colours are cast, be moved to and fro; for, by such motion, you will not only find, at what distance the whiteness is most perfect, but also see, how the colours gradually convene, and vanish into whiteness, and afterwards having crossed one another in that place where they compound Whiteness, are again dissipated, and severed, and in an inverted order retain the same colours, which they had before they entered the composition. You may also see, that, if any of the Colours at the *Lens* be intercepted, the Whiteness will be changed into the other colours. And therefore, that the composition of whiteness be perfect, care must be taken, that none of the colours fall besides the *Lens*.

In the annexed design of this Experiment, A B C expresseth the Prism set endwise to sight, close by the hole F of the window

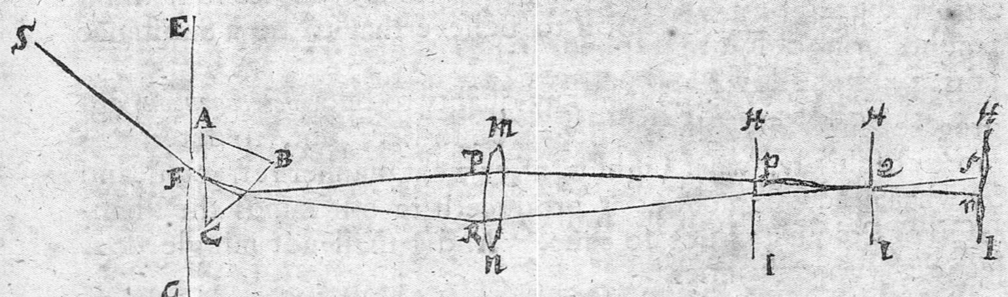

E G. Its vertical Angle A C B may conveniently be about 60 degrees: *M N* designeth the *Lens*. Its breadth $2\frac{1}{2}$ or 3 inches. S F one of the streight lines, in which difform Rays may be conceived to flow successively from the Sun. F P, and F R two of those Rays unequally refracted, which the *Lens* makes to converge towards Q, and after decussation to diverge again. And H I the paper, at divers distances, on which the colours are projected: which in Q constitute *Whiteness*, but are *Red* and *Yellow* in R, r, and ρ, and *Blew* and *Purple* in P, p, and π.

If

WORK BY HAND AND BRAIN

FIGURE 14
The prism experiment from Newton's first published paper on light and colours, University Library, T.340.1 b.85.6, pp. 3086-7.

Newton claimed that he had discovered the theory of light and colours in the early months of 1666. He demonstrated his idea that white light could be split into a spectrum of seven differently coloured and differently refrangible rays through a series of experiments with prisms. Although Newton described his optical theories in the first series of his Lucasian lectures, it seems likely that he had few hearers. His ideas reached a larger audience as a consequence of his design for a reflecting telescope. Isaac Barrow helped to communicate this to the Royal Society in 1671 and Newton then submitted a paper on light and colours to the Society's *Philosophical Transactions*. He became a fellow of the Royal Society in 1672 and was a frequent contributor to the *Philosophical Transactions*. John Collins, who assisted with the affairs of the Society, preserved many of Newton's letters from this time, and they later entered the Macclesfield Collection with the rest of Collins' papers. Newton was often anxious about both the costs of fellowship and the dangers of publicity, and withdrew from communication with the Society for several years after 1676. He also abandoned his plans to publish a complete account of his optical theories. These were resurrected by the success of the *Principia*. Newton's *Opticks* appeared in 1704 and a Latin translation with additional material was published in 1706. Newton incorporated those additions in the second, corrected edition of 1717.

20 *Philosophical Transactions*, NUMBER 80 (19 FEBRUARY 1672)
(figure 14)
4°: $4G$-$4I^{4}$
19.5 × 12 cm
Cambridge University Library, T.340.1 b.85.6

The first contact that Newton had with the wider world of natural philosophers outside Cambridge came at the instigation of Isaac

Barrow, who initiated a mathematical correspondence between Newton and John Collins (see catalogue number 38) in summer 1669. In November 1669, Newton visited London and met Collins for the first time. Collins soon learned something of Newton's latest invention, the reflecting telescope (see catalogue numbers 22–4), and it was probably through him that the Royal Society heard of the discovery at the end of 1671. Barrow again acted as an intermediary, bringing one of Newton's telescopes to London for the Society to inspect. Seth Ward, Bishop of Salisbury and formerly Savilian Professor of Astronomy at Oxford, immediately proposed Newton as a candidate for fellowship of the Society. He was elected a fellow of the Royal Society on 11 January 1672 and, on 18 January, promised the Society's secretary, Henry Oldenburg (1615–77), that he would send him 'an accompt of a Philosophicall discovery [which] induced mee to the making of the said Telescope' (see catalogue 24). This he did on 6 February, submitting the paper on light and colours that Oldenburg published on behalf of the Royal Society in his journal, the *Philosophical Transactions*, on 19 February 1672.

Newton had been involved with the publication of other men's works from the late 1660s, when he began helping Barrow with an edition of his lectures (see catalogue 32). This was, however, Newton's own first step into the harsh and competitive world of the communication of scientific discoveries. His experiences on this occasion perhaps helped to generate the suspicion with which he later regarded the printed word. Newton was at first eager to submit his work to the scrutiny of others. He welcomed Oldenburg's communication of his work to Christiaan Huygens, the pre-eminent natural philosopher of the age, then living in Paris. Yet, as praise for his work began to be tempered by questions about the theories that lay behind it, Newton began to realise some of the dangers of publicity. Correspondence with Oldenburg, and publication in the *Philosophical Transactions*, drew from Newton some of his most important optical discoveries and speculations, but it also put him increasingly on edge (see catalogue number 27).

The discoveries that Newton communicated in 1672 were not new to him, but were a summary of some of the main conclusions of his optical studies during the second half of the 1660s. In particular, his paper on light and colours contained an account (pp. 3086–7, on display) of his experiments with a prism to show that white light was composed of differently refrangible rays of coloured light, forming a spectrum from purple to red. Yet the confidence and familiarity with which Newton presented his results may have been one of the reasons for the scepticism that greeted many of his findings. Several prominent natural philosophers, in particular Huygens, Robert Hooke, and Ignace Gaston Pardies, soon engaged Newton in a wide-ranging correspondence, mediated through Oldenburg, that questioned both the conclusions and the methods of Newton's optical experiments.

H. W. Turnbull, J.F. Scott, A.R. Hall and Laura Tilling (eds), *The Correspondence of Isaac Newton*, 7 vols (Cambridge, 1959–77), vol. 1, especially pp. 74–107. Richard S. Westfall, *Never at Rest. A Biography of Isaac Newton* (Cambridge, 1980), pp. 231–80; I. Bernard Cohen (ed.), *Isaac Newton's Papers & Letters on Natural Philosophy* (Cambridge, 1958), pp. 47–59 (which reprints Newton's paper).

21 WHIPPLE MUSEUM, CAMBRIDGE, ACCESSION NUMBER 1254
60° glass prism

One of the causes of the hostile reaction to Newton's theory of light and colours was the manner of Newton's account of his experiments with prisms. This gave the impression of being a simple, historical narrative of actions, beginning early in 1666, that were both easy to perform and straightforward to repeat. But Newton was being disingenuous both in terms of historical detail and with reference to the ease with which another might see what he had seen. Accounts in one of Newton's notebooks (see catalogue number 3) show that he bought lenses and grinding tools in April 1667 and three prisms in spring 1668. Experiments recorded in Newton's other notebooks (see catalogue numbers 9 and 11) suggest that he had begun using prisms some time before this as a means of exploring the optical theories of Descartes and others. It seems likely that Newton's initial discoveries can be dated to autumn 1665. But the path that Newton took was nevertheless slower and more complicated than he later suggested. Many of Newton's contemporaries had looked through prisms. His discovery depended on the experiment in which he allowed a sunbeam to traverse the prism, casting the spectrum onto the opposite wall of his room. In addition to this, his argument about the composition of light turned on an 'experimentum crucis' in which a second prism was used to demonstrate that the differently coloured rays that made up white light were independent of the angle at which the light had initially struck the first prism.

Despite Newton's account, the circumstances of his experiments remain unclear and they certainly puzzled his contemporaries. Most puzzling of all was Newton's description of the spectrum itself. He initially suggested that it contained five distinct colours, later modifying this number to seven. Yet the distinction between these colours was understandably obscure to Newton's readers. Since Newton was himself uncertain about the causes of the behaviour of light that he had observed, it is not surprising that many of his contemporaries should have been sceptical about both his findings and the explanations that he offered for them.

As a result of doubts about the conduct of his experiments, Newton described the prisms that he used in some detail, particularly in later correspondence. They were all triangular prisms each of whose angles was close to 60°. A number of candidates have been proposed as surviving examples of Newton's prisms. These include the prism on display. However, none of these prisms in fact match the exact dimensions that Newton specified. Indeed, it seems likely that they are all of much later manufacture, and that the prism on display is one that was presented to the Cavendish Laboratory in 1876 from the collection of W.H. Wollaston.

A.A. Mills, 'Newton's Prisms and his Experiments on the Spectrum', *Notes and Records of the Royal Society of London*, 36 (1981–2), 13–36; Simon Schaffer, 'Glass Works: Newton's Prisms and the Uses of Experiment', in David Gooding, Trevor Pinch and Simon Schaffer (eds), *The Uses of Experiment* (Cambridge, 1989), pp. 67–104; J.A. Lohne, 'Isaac Newton: The Rise of a Scientist 1661–1671', *Notes and Records of the Royal Society of London*, 20 (1965), 125–39.

22 CAMBRIDGE UNIVERSITY LIBRARY, MS. ADD. 3970, ff. 591r- 592v

(figures 15 & 16)

24.4 × 37 cm

The telescopes which were responsible for the remarkable discoveries of Galileo and other seventeenth-century astronomers all depended on the ability of lenses to bring objects closer to the observer through the refraction of light. They suffered from a number of limitations that contemporaries hoped might be alleviated through new discoveries. Newton's essay 'Of Refractions' (see catalogue number 9) considered solutions to one of these limitations, spherical aberration, through the grinding of non-spherical lenses. His work on light, however, suggested

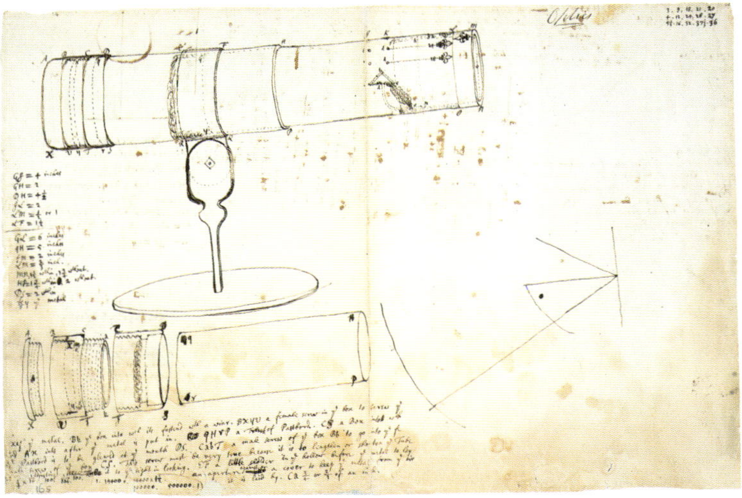

FIGURE 15
Drawing by Newton of his reflecting telescope and its parts, University Library, Ms. Add. 3970, ff. 591r–592v.

that another problem, the distortion in colour and clarity of a distant object viewed through several lenses (chromatic aberration), might be more difficult to solve.

One way to overcome this problem was to use a mirror instead of a lens to gather light into the telescope. The construction of a reflecting telescope had the additional advantage of avoiding the problems of focussing an image resulting from spherical aberration. By 1668, Newton already possessed suitable tools and experience in working metal and glass to manufacture a reflecting telescope. He gave an account of his invention in his first surviving letter (a copy of which was later made by John Collins and is now in the Macclesfield Collection) in February 1669. Soon afterwards, Newton discussed his telescope with instrument makers in London and with Collins. Following his election to the Royal Society, Newton composed a paper about his telescope for the *Philosophical Transactions* (number 81, 25 March 1672, 4004–10, see figure 16). This described the instrument's construction, which Newton had already committed to paper in the drawing on display. The telescope's tube was made of pasteboard and was lengthened and shortened for focussing by means of metal screws. There were two highly polished mirrors of copper: one concave at the closed end of the telescope to reflect an object, the other small and flat, placed at the opposite end of the telescope to direct the reflected rays of light towards a tiny glass lens

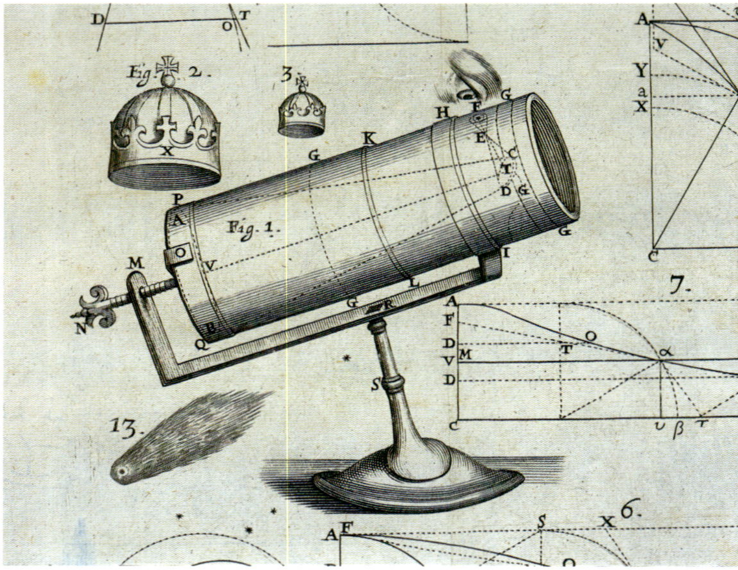

FIGURE 16
Newton's reflecting telescope, which doubled the size of a crown from a weather-cock on a neighbouring tower when compared with observations using a standard refracting telescope, University Library, T.340.1 b.85.7, table 1.

near the opening of the tube, where the enlarged image could be viewed by an observer.

Like his other optical discoveries, Newton's telescope generated controversy. It was clear that it could achieve a remarkable level of magnification compared with refracting telescopes of a similar size. Despite this, Huygens rightly wondered about the difficulty of manufacturing mirrors of suitable smoothness for the instrument and preventing them from tarnishing. Others, including Hooke, claimed that they had already described similar telescopes themselves and that therefore Newton deserved little credit for his work. It was certainly the case that James Gregory had already published another, more manageable, design of reflecting telescope, and that this model later became the standard for manufacture. Newton himself did not abandon the hope of improving refracting telescopes, which in fact remained the principal tools for late seventeenth-century astronomy. He nevertheless continued to develop his reflecting telescope in response to his critics. In March 1672, he suggested the replacement of the secondary, plane mirror with a prism. Although he did not ever build a telescope with this improvement, he did make a drawing of one, which is displayed here. This was also the design that Newton later described in the *Opticks* (1704).

H. W. Turnbull, J.F. Scott, A.R. Hall and Laura Tilling (eds), *The Correspondence of Isaac Newton*, 7 vols (Cambridge, 1959–77), vol. 1, 3–9, 72–7, 126–30; I. Bernard Cohen, 'Newton's Description of the Reflecting Telescope', *Notes and Records of the Royal Society of London*, 47 (1993), 1–9; A. Rupert Hall, 'John Collins on Newton's Telescope', *Notes and Records of the Royal Society of London*, 49 (1995), 71–8.

Presented to Cambridge University Library by the fifth Earl of Portsmouth. See *A Catalogue of the Portsmouth Collection of Books and Papers written by or belonging to Sir Isaac Newton* (Cambridge, 1888), pp. 9–10.

23 WHIPPLE MUSEUM, CAMBRIDGE, ACCESSION NUMBER 2662

Replica of Newton's reflecting telescope

This is a replica made in 1953 of a reflecting telescope in the possession of the Royal Society. Newton had deposited one of his telescopes with the Royal Society at the end of 1671. This was placed in the Society's Repository, or museum, where it remained until at least 1718, although the Society had changed its address several times in the intervening years. When the Repository was catalogued in 1731, however, only the two mirrors remained. These had also disappeared by 1827. The replica on display is based on a telescope given to the Royal Society in 1766 by the London instrument makers, Thomas Heath and Tycho Wing. This telescope bears signs of restoration during the eighteenth century but was probably made by Newton in 1671. Newton constructed two telescopes in that year. One he sent to the Royal Society, the other he built with his friend John Wickens, who shared his rooms in Trinity. Newton kept this second telescope until at least the 1690s.

A. Rupert Hall and A.D.C. Simpson, 'An Account of the Royal Society's Newton Telescope', *Notes and Records of the Royal Society of London*, 50 (1996), 1–11; A.D.C. Simpson, 'Newton's Telescope and the Cataloguing of the Royal Society's Repository', *Notes and Records of the Royal Society of London*, 38 (1983–4), 187–214; A.A. Mills and P.J. Turvey, 'Newton's Telescope. An Examination of the Reflecting Telescope attributed to Sir Isaac Newton in the Possession of the Royal Society', *Notes and Records of the Royal Society of London*, 33 (1978–9), 133– 55.

24 CAMBRIDGE UNIVERSITY LIBRARY, MACCLESFIELD COLLECTION, BOX 3/4/13

20.4 × 15.7

This is the second letter that Newton wrote to Henry Oldenburg, and the first following his election to the Royal Society. In an earlier letter of 6 January (also in the Macclesfield Collection), he had thanked

Oldenburg for his care in securing Newton's priority for the invention of the reflecting telescope. In this letter, which Oldenburg received on 19 January, Newton considered possible improvements to the metal mirrors that he had used in the telescope. This discussion revealed the considerable understanding of how to work metal and make alloys that Newton had gained since the start of his alchemical experiments in the late 1660s. Newton concluded his letter by asking about the duties of a Fellow of the Royal Society and for information about the Society's meetings. In formulating these queries, he promised to send the Society an account of his theory of light and colours, which had prompted him to construct his telescope and '[which] I doubt not but will prove much more gratefull then the communication of that instrument, being in my Judgment the oddest if not the most considerable detection [which] hath hitherto beene made in the operations of Nature' (see catalogue number 20).

H. W. Turnbull, J.F. Scott, A.R. Hall and Laura Tilling (eds), *The Correspondence of Isaac Newton*, 7 vols (Cambridge, 1959–77), vol. 1, 82–3 (which prints this letter).

Purchased from the Macclesfield family by Cambridge University Library, August 2000.

25 CAMBRIDGE UNIVERSITY LIBRARY, MACCLESFIELD COLLECTION, BOX 3/4/22
(figure 17)
20.7 × 15.6 cm

This is one of numerous letters exchanged between Newton and Oldenburg in the aftermath of Newton's first publications in the *Philosophical Transactions*. Oldenburg had written to Newton on 2 July 1672, passing on encouragement and criticism from a letter that Huygens had sent on 21 June. Newton's reply was composed at Stoke on 8 July. He acknowledged Huygens' remarks and asked about the progress of Christopher Cock, a London instrument maker, who was building a four-foot reflecting telescope with metal mirrors and also making trials of much shorter telescopes, such as Newton's own prototype. The Royal Society had asked Cock to make a larger version of Newton's telescope on 14 March. Despite his confidence that it would be completed within two weeks, Cock had been forced to report a month later that he was having trouble burnishing the large steel mirror

FIGURE 17
A letter from Oldenburg discussing reactions to Newton's papers on light and on the reflecting telescope, University Library, Macclesfield Collection, Box 3/4/22.

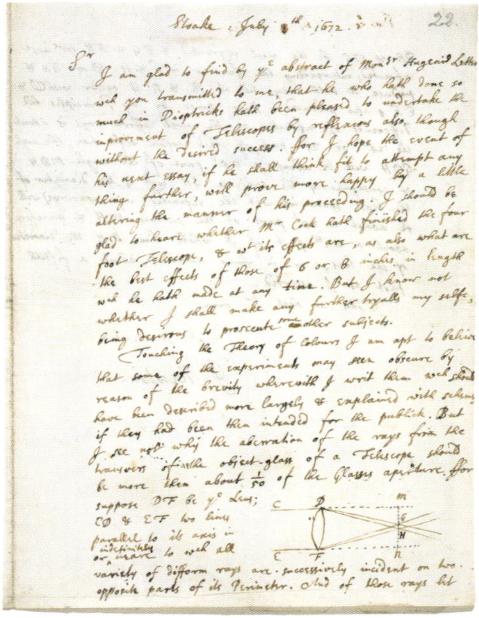
Stoake : July 8th 1672. 22.

Sr

I am glad to find by ye abstract of Monsr Hugenius Letter wch you transmitted to me, that he who hath done so much in Diopthicks hath been pleased to undertake the improvement of Telescopes by reflexions also, though without the desired success. For I hope the event of his next essay, if he shall think fit to attempt any thing further, will prove more happy by a little altering the manner of his proceeding. I should be glad to heare whether Mr Cook hath finished the four foot Telescope, & wt its effects are, as also what are the best effects of those of 6 or 8 inches in length wch he hath made at any time. But I know not whether I shall make any further tryalls my selfe, being desirous to prosecute some other subjects.

Touching the Theory of Colours I am apt to beleive that some of the experiments may seem obscure by reason of the brevity wherewith I writ them wch should have been described more largely & explained with schemes if they had been then intended for the publick. But I see not why the aberration of the rays from the transvers of the object-glass of a Telescope should be more then about $\frac{1}{50}$ of the Glasses aperture. For suppose DF be ye Lens; CD & EF two lines parallel to its axis in or neare to wch all indefinitely variety of difform rays are successively incident on two opposite parts of its Perimeter. And of those rays let

that the telescope required. Newton was already becoming bored with the detailed investigation of his invention and its potential, which seemed to be generating more and more criticism of his design. As a result, he commented 'I know not whether I shall make any further tryalls my selfe, being desirous to prosecute some other subjects'. The letter concluded with a discussion of spherical aberration in telescopes, in which Newton tried to clarify parts of his theory of light and colours. On this topic, Newton was still willing to give ground to Huygens and other critics, admitting that 'I am apt to beleive that some of the experiments may seem obscure by reason of the brevity wherewith I writ them'. Nevertheless, he maintained that his measurements, which Huygens had doubted, were accurate.

H. W. Turnbull, J.F. Scott, A.R. Hall and Laura Tilling (eds), *The Correspondence of Isaac Newton*, 7 vols (Cambridge, 1959–77), vol. 1, 212–13 (which prints this letter); A. Rupert and Marie Boas Hall (eds), *The Correspondence of Henry Oldenburg*, 13 vols (Madison and London, 1965–86), vol. 9, 116–25, 150–1; Thomas Birch (ed.), *The History of the Royal Society of London*, 4 vols (London, 1756–7), vol. 3, pp. 19, 43.

Purchased from the Macclesfield family by Cambridge University Library, August 2000.

26 CAMBRIDGE UNIVERSITY LIBRARY, MS. ADD. 3970 f. 501r

(figure 18)

31.3 × 20 cm

The debate over Newton's theory of light and colours continued throughout the early 1670s, encouraged partly by Oldenburg's indefatigable pursuit of communications for the Royal Society. On 7 December 1675, Newton sent Oldenburg the most complete answer that he had yet composed to his critics, in the form of two documents, 'An Hypothesis explaining the Properties of Light discoursed of in my severall papers' and the 'Discourse of Observations'. Both papers were based partly on drafts that Newton had composed in 1672. They were read aloud at the weekly meetings of the Royal Society held between 9 December 1675 and 10 February 1676, and constituted the majority of the business on those occasions. The purpose of Newton's 'Hypothesis' (see catalogue number 28) was to try to expand on the theory of light and colours in order to explain the causes of the behaviour that Newton had described. It was a direct response to Robert Hooke and others who

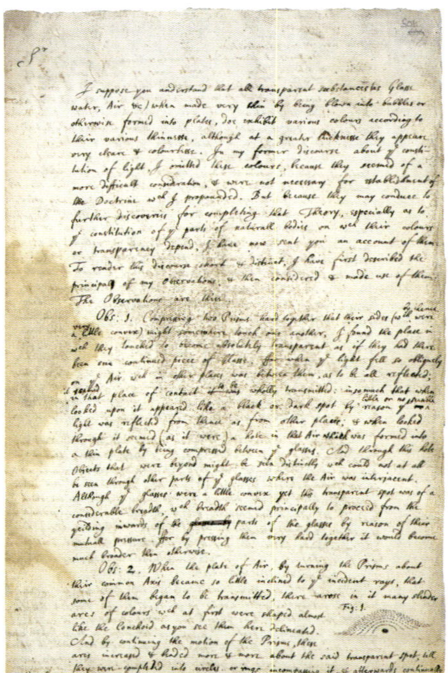

FIGURE 18
Newton's observation of coloured rings produced by light passing through a thin film of air between two glass plates, University Library, Ms. Add. 3970, f. 501r.

supported the theory that colour was produced by the modification of light as it fell on particular bodies. Despite the rejection of this position that his theory entailed, Newton was still drawn to many aspects of a mechanical explanation for light. He struggled to find a cause for the changes of state that light appeared to undergo as it was transmitted across the boundaries between different media. In the end, he argued for the existence of a pervasive form of subtle matter, or aether, that might produce these effects both mechanically and through some form of spiritual action, perhaps implanted by God. This argument married Newton's continuing respect for Cartesian natural philosophy with his growing conviction, nurtured by alchemical study, that organic as well as mechanical explanations were necessary for an understanding of growth and change in nature.

In both the 'Hypothesis' and the 'Discourse of Observations', Newton drew on the optical and anatomical experiments that he had carried out in the mid-1660s (see catalogue number 11). The 'Discourse of Observations', of which the manuscript on display is a fair copy in Newton's hand, was concerned primarily with the behaviour of light as it passed through thin films of air or water between two glass plates. It consisted of twenty-four observations, with careful measurements, that helped to establish that the transmission of light was periodic in character. Inconveniently, this was exactly what Hooke had argued. Newton's experiments had been greatly influenced by Hooke's work on colour in *Micrographia* (1665) but his own theory involved a rejection of many of Hooke's ideas. Rather than regarding his findings as exceptional, however, Newton used them as the cornerstone of his new ideas of the transmission of light. They provided a firm, empirical case for what was otherwise a largely speculative argument.

In January 1676, Newton changed his mind about allowing Oldenburg to publish his most recent thoughts about light. Perhaps defeated by the difficulty of propounding a coherent theory, Newton abandoned his optical writing for over a decade. Yet there were also other reasons for his silence. The awkwardness of his personal circumstances (see catalogue number 5) encouraged him to avoid controversy. He was also beginning to have doubts about Oldenburg's reliability as a mediator between author and critics. When he did start to draft the text of the *Opticks* in 1687–8, Newton incorporated the 'Discourse of Observations' almost without change into Book II. As he struggled to complete the work in the early 1690s, however, he returned to the hypotheses that he had first introduced in 1672 and had developed extensively in 1675. By the mid-1690s, he had extended his theory of the transmission of light to cover thick plates as well as thin films. Nevertheless, an adequate physical explanation for the behaviour of light continued to elude him even in the composition of the Queries for the *Opticks* in the final years before the book's publication in 1704.

H. W. Turnbull, J.F. Scott, A.R. Hall and Laura Tilling (eds), *The Correspondence of Isaac Newton*, 7 vols (Cambridge, 1959–77), vol. 1, 110–16, 360–92; Cambridge University Library, Ms. Add. 3970, ff. 519r–28v; Thomas Birch (ed.), *The History of the Royal Society of London*, 4 vols (London, 1756–7), vol. 3, 247–305; I. Bernard Cohen (ed.), *Isaac Newton's Papers and Letters on Natural Philosophy* (Cambridge, 1958), pp. 177–235 (which reprints the text of the 'Hypothesis' and the 'Discourse of Observations' from Birch); Alan E. Shapiro, *Fits, Passions, and Paroxysms* (Cambridge, 1993), pp. 49–97, 138–50.

Presented to Cambridge University Library by the fifth Earl of Portsmouth. See *A Catalogue of the Portsmouth Collection of Books and Papers written by or belonging to Sir Isaac Newton* (Cambridge, 1888), pp. 9–10.

27 CAMBRIDGE UNIVERSITY LIBRARY, MACCLESFIELD COLLECTION, BOX 3/4/18

31 × 20.5 cm

This is a letter that Newton sent to John Collins (see catalogue number 38) on 25 May 1672. It replied to a typical letter that Collins had written on 30 April (also in the Macclesfield Collection), which contained extensive news of books that were printing in London and overseas. In the first flush of his fame, Newton had had ambitious plans for publications. He now informed Collins that the edition that he had prepared of the *Geographia universalis* of Bernhard Varenius was ready for the press, as were the additions that he had written for Nicolaus Mercator's edition of Gerard Kinckhuysen's *Algebra*. Newton's edition of Varenius was indeed published in 1672, but Collins was less successful in coaxing any of Newton's mathematical work into the world. Already Newton had decided not to prepare an edition of his optical lectures (see catalogue number 6) for publication: 'finding... by the little use I have made of the Presse, that I shall not enjoy my former serene liberty till I have done with it'. The reaction to his paper on light and colours, particularly from Hooke and other natural philosophers that he had admired when he had known them only through their books, had convinced Newton of the dangers of publicity. He worried about the treatment of his ideas in the *Philosophical Transactions*. Although he was given the opportunity to reply several times to his critics, he told Collins that he was 'a little troubled to find my selfe cut short of that fredome of communication [which] I hoped to enjoy, but cannot any longer without giving offence to some persons whome I have ever respected'. In March 1673, Oldenburg had to talk Newton out of resigning from the Royal Society. Newton chafed continually against the fees that he had to pay. The lengthy trial by correspondence, which lasted until his withdrawal from the Royal Society in 1676, only served to confirm the disillusionment and insecurity that were already apparent in summer 1672.

H. W. Turnbull, J.F. Scott, A.R. Hall and Laura Tilling (eds), *The Correspondence of Isaac Newton*, 7 vols (Cambridge, 1959–77), vol. 1, 146–50, 151–2 (which prints this letter).

Purchased from the Earl of Macclesfield by Cambridge University Library, August 2000.

28 CAMBRIDGE UNIVERSITY LIBRARY, MS. ADD. 3970, ff. 544r-545v
(figure 19)
29.9 × 18.6 cm

Newton composed 'An Hypothesis explaining the Properties of Light discoursed of in my severall papers' as an answer to Robert Hooke's 'Considerations' on the new theory of light and colours (see catalogue number 26). He developed his initial reply of November 1672 into the more complete document that he sent to Henry Oldenburg in December 1675.

The pages on display provide evidence of Newton's care in constructing optical experiments that would allow him to measure the phenomena that he observed. They illustrate his attempts to use quantification to support the conclusions of his theory of light and colours and assist in finding causes for the behaviour of light. Like Descartes, Newton argued that this behaviour was the result of interactions between corpuscles of light and the particles of the medium through which they travelled. He suggested that light itself might excite vibrations in an aetherial medium, and drew a comparison between effects of the colours of the spectrum and those of the divisions of a string necessary to sound the tones of a musical scale. This analogy had already led Newton to define seven colours in the spectrum, where he had earlier

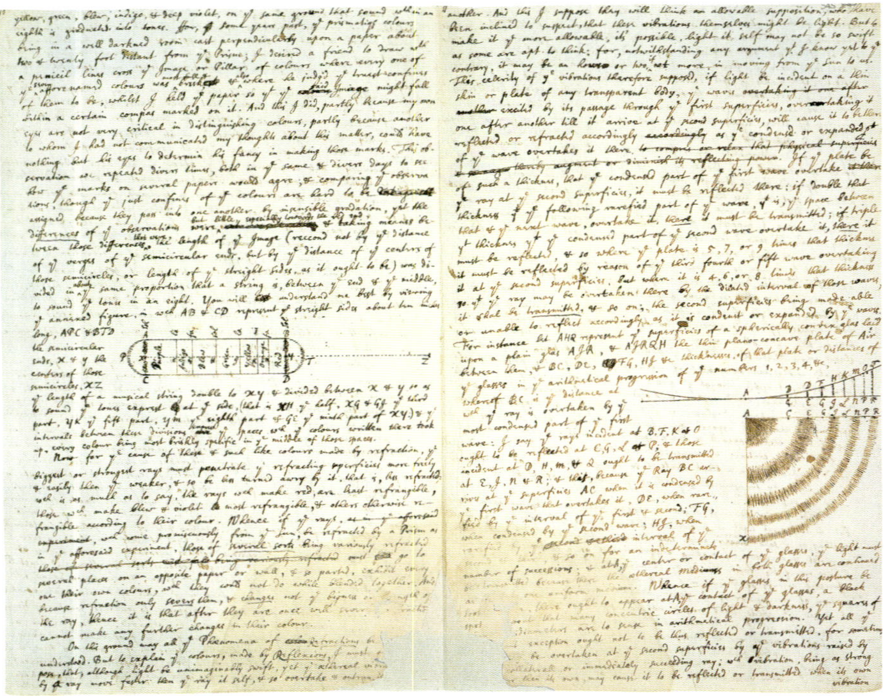

FIGURE 19
Newton's attempt to calibrate light as a vibration in an aetherial medium, similar to the calibration of sound travelling through the air as represented in a musical scale, University Library, Ms. Add. 3970, ff. 544r–545v.

seen only five. But, unlike Hooke, Newton was convinced that light was propagated as particles moving in straight lines and not as a wave. His experiments with thin films created difficulties for any explanation of the phenomena based simply on the velocity of light. In order to explain the rings that he had observed, Newton was tempted to argue that the vibrations set up as light passed through a medium exceeded the speed of light itself. As in the analogy with a musical scale, Newton suggested that it was the size of particles of light that determined the effects that were visible both as different colours and as patterns of interference. The observations that he presented in support of this analysis later formed the basis for the puzzling theory of 'fits of easy reflection and transmission' that Newton developed in the *Opticks*.

Penelope Gouk, *Music, Science and Natural Magic in Seventeenth-Century England* (New Haven, 1999), pp. 241–6.

Presented to Cambridge University Library by the fifth Earl of Portsmouth. See *A Catalogue of the Portsmouth Collection of Books and Papers written by or belonging to Sir Isaac Newton* (Cambridge, 1888), pp. 9–10.

29 ISAAC NEWTON, *Opticks*
(London, 1704)
(figure 20)
4°: A^{4}, B^{1-3}; B^{3-4}; $C-S^{4}$; $2A-2S^{4}$; $2T^{1}$
Cambridge University Library, shelfmark Adv. b. 39.3

Newton took great care in the preparation of the *Opticks* for the press. This was partly a result of the anxiety that he continued to feel about some of his conclusions, which resulted in the suppression of the introduction that he had planned and the curtailment and redistribution of the fourth book of the text. The search for a cause of the behaviour of light continued to vex Newton. His last minute corrections are often apparent in the printers' copy of the first edition (Ms. Add. 3970(3)). Further revisions were made impossible by the publication of the book in 1704. However, Newton continued to work at the text. His additions to what appear to be proof sheets, for Books I and II and most of Book III, are displayed here. Drafts of these corrections also survive in the manuscript of the *Opticks* (Ms. Add. 3970(3), f. 240b, for example, incorporates the material that Newton added to Query 10 on page 134 of the proofs). Newton saw the need for a second edition of the book almost immediately and commissioned his friend and disciple, Samuel Clarke

FIGURE 20
Proofs of the first edition of the *Opticks*, showing the corrections that Newton made in preparing the second edition, University Library, shelfmark Adv. b. 39.3, pp. 134-5.

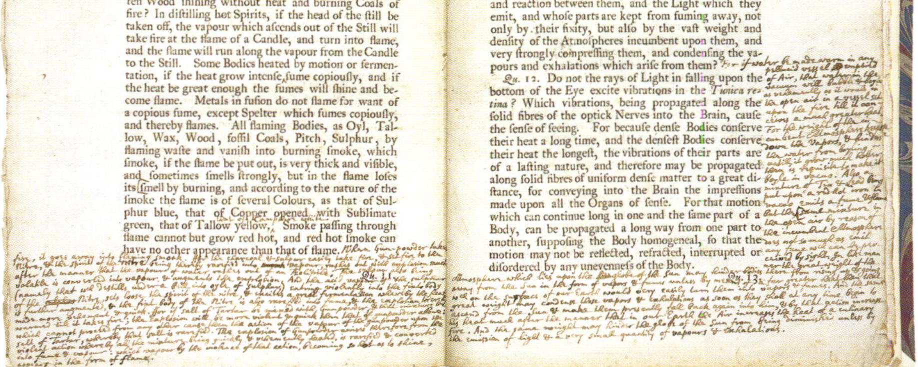
[134]

Qu. 9. Is not fire a Body heated ſo hot as to emit Light copiouſly? For what elſe is a red hot Iron than fire? And what elſe is a burning Coal than red hot Wood?

Qu. 10. Is not flame a vapour, fume or exhalation heated red hot, that is, ſo hot as to ſhine? For Bodies do not flame without emitting a copious fume, and this fume burns in the flame. The *Ignis Fatuus* is a vapour ſhining without heat, and is there not the ſame difference between this vapour and flame, as between rotten Wood ſhining without heat and burning Coals of fire? In diſtilling hot Spirits, if the head of the ſtill be taken off, the vapour which aſcends out of the Still will take fire at the flame of a Candle, and turn into flame, and the flame will run along the vapour from the Candle to the Still. Some Bodies heated by motion or fermentation, if the heat grow intenſe, fume copiouſly, and if the heat be great enough the fumes will ſhine and become flame. Metals in fuſion do not flame for want of a copious fume, except Spelter which fumes copiouſly, and thereby flames. All flaming Bodies, as Oyl, Tallow, Wax, Wood, foſſil Coals, Pitch, Sulphur, by flaming waſte and vaniſh into burning ſmoke, which ſmoke, if the flame be put out, is very thick and viſible, and ſometimes ſmells ſtrongly, but in the flame loſes its ſmell by burning, and according to the nature of the ſmoke the flame is of ſeveral Colours, as that of Sulphur blue, that of Copper opened with Sublimate green, that of Tallow yellow. Smoke paſſing through flame cannot but grow red hot, and red hot ſmoke can have no other appearance than that of flame.

[135]

Qu. 11. Do not great Bodies conſerve their heat the longeſt, their parts heating one another, and may not great denſe and fix'd Bodies, when heated beyond a certain degree, emit Light ſo copiouſly, as by the emiſſion and reaction of its Light, and the reflexions and refractions of its rays within its pores to grow ſtill hotter, till it comes to a certain period of heat, ſuch as is that of the Sun? And are not the Sun and fix'd Stars great Earths vehemently hot, whoſe heat is conſerved by the greatneſs of the Bodies, and the mutual action and reaction between them, and the Light which they emit, and whoſe parts are kept from fuming away, not only by their fixity, but alſo by the vaſt weight and denſity of the Atmoſpheres incumbent upon them, and very ſtrongly compreſſing them, and condenſing the vapours and exhalations which ariſe from them?

Qu. 12. Do not the rays of Light in falling upon the bottom of the Eye excite vibrations in the *Tunica retina*? Which vibrations, being propagated along the ſolid fibres of the optick Nerves into the Brain, cauſe the ſenſe of ſeeing. For becauſe denſe Bodies conſerve their heat a long time, and the denſeſt Bodies conſerve their heat the longeſt, the vibrations of their parts are of a laſting nature, and therefore may be propagated along ſolid fibres of uniform denſe matter to a great diſtance, for conveying into the Brain the impreſſions made upon all the Organs of ſenſe. For that motion which can continue long in one and the ſame part of a Body, can be propagated a long way from one part to another, ſuppoſing the Body homogeneal, ſo that the motion may not be reflected, refracted, interrupted or diſordered by any unevenneſs of the Body.

(1675–1729), to make a Latin translation that would include some of the new work.

Richard S. Westfall, *Never at Rest. A Biography of Isaac Newton* (Cambridge, 1980), pp. 643–8.

Presented to Cambridge University Library by the fifth Earl of Portsmouth. See *A Catalogue of the Portsmouth Collection of Books and Papers written by or belonging to Sir Isaac Newton* (Cambridge, 1888), p. 41.

30 ISAAC NEWTON, *Optice*, TRANS. SAMUEL CLARKE
(London, 1706)
4°: A^4, b^3, A–3S^4, 3T^2
19 × 12.5
Cambridge University Library, shelfmark Adv. b. 39.4

Clarke was paid £500 for translating the *Opticks* into Latin. Another young friend of Newton, the mathematical tutor Abraham De Moivre saw the book through the press. It included a number of changes, most importantly the addition of seven new queries at the end of Book III, explaining some of Newton's thoughts about the nature of matter and the action of light and gravity. Further queries were introduced into the second English edition of the *Opticks*, which appeared in 1717.

This copy of *Optice* belonged to Newton and includes a few corrections in his hand, especially to the list of errata (sig. b1r-3v). Newton also turned down the corners of some of its pages to mark passages that featured in later controversies concerning his work. The book is open to display illustrations based on Newton's earlier optical experiments.

John Harrison, *The Library of Isaac Newton* (Cambridge, 1978), p. 201.

Listed by the booksellers who appraised Newton's library for his executors; bought with the rest of the library by John Huggins in 1727. Bookplate of Charles Huggins. Bookplate of James Musgrave, with shelfmark E6–27. Presumed sold at Thame Park, 13–15 January 1920. Bought by C.W. Adams from Thomas Thorp, Guildford, for 16s. in July 1921. Presented by Adams to Cambridge University Library, 8 December 1928.

CALCULATION AND CONTROVERSY

The young Newton owed his greatest intellectual debt to the French mathematician and natural philosopher, René Descartes. He was influenced by both English and Continental commentators on Descartes' work. Problems derived from the writings of the Oxford mathematician, John Wallis, also featured strongly in Newton's development as a mathematician capable of handling infinite series and the complexities of calculations involving curved lines. The 'Waste Book' that Newton used for much of his mathematical working in the 1660s demonstrates how quickly his talents surpassed those of most of his contemporaries. Nevertheless, the evolution of Newton's thought was only possible through consideration of what his immediate predecessors had already achieved. Once Newton had become a public figure, however, he became increasingly concerned to ensure proper recognition for his own ideas. In the quarrels that resulted with mathematicians like Gottfried Wilhelm Leibniz (1646–1716) or Johann Bernoulli (1667–1748), Newton supervised his disciples in the reconstruction of the historical record of his discoveries. One of those followers was William Jones, tutor to the future Earl of Macclesfield, who acquired or copied many letters and papers relating to Newton's early career. These formed the heart of the Macclesfield Collection, which has recently been purchased by Cambridge University Library.

31 RENÉ DESCARTES, *Geometria* ED. AND TRANS. FRANS VAN SCHOOTEN
2 parts (Amsterdam, 1659–61)
4°: $\ast$-2$\ast^4$, A-3T^4, G-3G^4; π^2, $\ast$-2$\ast^4$, A-F^4
Trinity College, Cambridge, shelfmark NQ 16/203

Newton acquired this book 'a little before Christmas' 1664, having read an earlier edition of Descartes' *Geometry* by van Schooten earlier in the year. His study of Descartes in the mid-1660s shaped his development as a mathematician and natural philosopher (see catalogue number 3 for further discussion of this book). For many years, he continued to believe that his work was compatible with Descartes' ideas. It seems likely that Newton's real break with Cartesianism took place only in the 1680s. The consideration of the nature of gravity and the successful creation of his own system of celestial mechanics in those years brought Newton firmly to different conclusions from Descartes.

Despite his early achievements as a mathematician, Newton seems to have had relatively little knowledge of classical geometry, other than Euclid's *Elements*, before the late 1670s. Then, he embarked on a close study of the writings of Pappus of Alexandria. He may have been prompted to do this by an increasing interest in classical authors and ancient wisdom, although that only reached its height a decade later. Equally, the publication of new studies of classical geometry, particularly Pierre Fermat's work on Apollonius, which appeared in 1679, may have caught Newton's attention. More probably, however, his curiosity was sparked by some remarks that he had found when reviewing the edition of Descartes' *Geometria* that he had used as a young man, with an eye to deploying it in the lectures on algebra that he was now delivering in Cambridge. Certainly, Newton marked a number of places in his copy of the *Geometria* with the words 'Error', 'non probo', 'Non Geom.', and 'Imperf.'. These annotations all seem to relate to Descartes' misrepresentation of Pappus' conics. Newton expanded on his criticism in a manuscript entitled 'Errores Cartesii Geometriae' (Ms. Add. 3961(4), f. 23r-4r), in which he considered Descartes' mistakes in detail.

D.T. Whiteside (ed.), *The Mathematical Papers of Isaac Newton*, 8 vols (Cambridge, 1967–81), vol. 4, 218–29, 336–45; John Harrison, *The Library of Isaac Newton* (Cambridge, 1978), pp. 14–15, 132.

Newton's signature appears on the stub of one of the flyleaves at the front of the book, which was later owned by John Smith. Bequeathed by his son, Robert Smith (1689–1768), who was Master of Trinity.

32 ISAAC BARROW, *Lectiones XVIII*, ED. ISAAC NEWTON
2 parts (London, 1669–70)
4°: A⁴, a², B-R⁴; A-T², V⁴
17 × 11.5 cm
Trinity College, Cambridge, shelfmark NQ 16/181

During his own lifetime, Isaac Barrow published two volumes of lectures that he had delivered as Lucasian Professor. His optical lectures appeared in November 1669 and those on geometry in summer 1670. Shortly after the publication of the second volume, Barrow presented a copy of both sets of lectures to Newton, who had assisted him in preparing them for the press. Newton dated the gift 'July 7th 1670' in the inscription that he wrote beside the titlepage, although he appears initially to have written the month as 'August'.

John Harrison, *The Library of Isaac Newton* (Cambridge, 1978), p. 94.

Listed by the booksellers who appraised Newton's library for his executors; bought with the rest of the library by John Huggins in 1727. Bookplate of Charles Huggins. Bookplate of James Musgrave, with shelfmark B1–20. Presented to Trinity College, Cambridge, on 30 October 1943 by the Pilgrim Trust.

33 CAMBRIDGE UNIVERSITY LIBRARY, MS. ADD. 4004, ff. 32v–33r
(figure 21)
31 × 20.8 cm
Manuscript of 196 numbered folios, extracted from a larger volume.
Modern binding.

The most cherished legacy that Newton received from his stepfather, Barnabas Smith (1582–1653), seems to have been a vast manuscript commonplace book. Smith was rector of North Witham, a wealthy clergyman who married Newton's mother on 27 January 1646. The immediate consequence of this union was that the three-year-old Isaac Newton had to be sent to live with his grandmother. On Smith's death, Newton appears to have inherited his library, most of which he gave away much later in life to a kinsman in Grantham. Smith himself had made extensive use of these books, in compiling a volume of theological commonplaces. This consisted of hundreds of folios bound in pasteboard, ruled at the top and in the margin of each folio to allow space for a heading and references to each entry. Newton was not interested by the very pedestrian efforts in divinity, largely the culling of quotations, with which Smith had begun to fill the book since its inception on 12 May 1612. He wanted its paper, as the title that he wrote on its original cover in February 1664 ('Waste Book') suggested.

By September 1664, Newton had started to use some of the pages for the optical and mathematical calculations, inspired by Descartes and van Schooten, that were beginning to occupy him (see catalogue numbers 2–3). Over the next two years, Newton broadened his reading only slightly. Nevertheless, through the study of Wallis' works and of

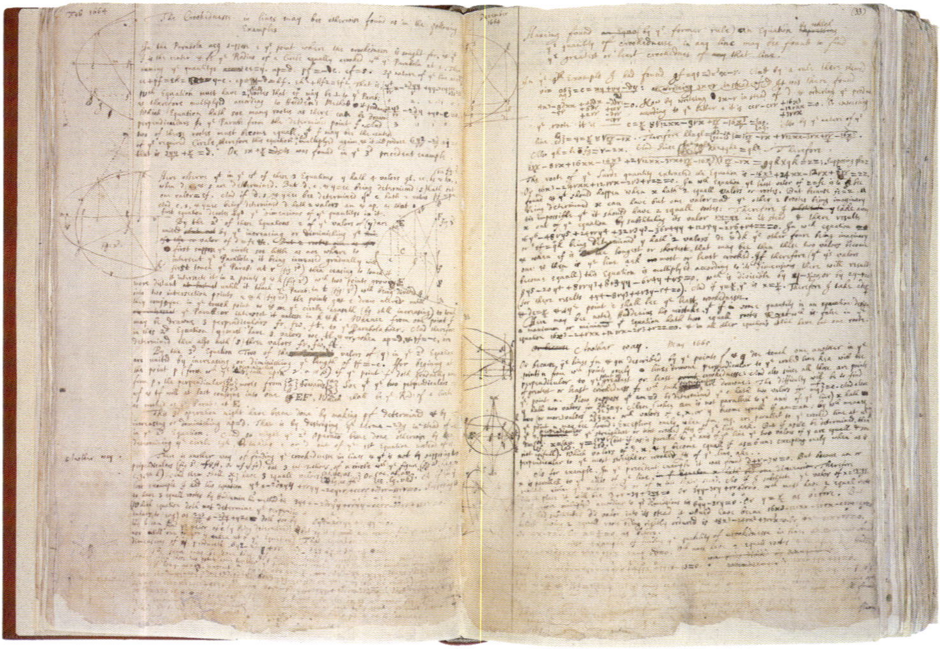

FIGURE 21
En route to the calculus, entries in Newton's 'Waste Book' from 1665, University Library, Ms. Add. 4004, ff. 32v–33r.

the other authors (Johannes Hudde, Hendrick van Heuraet, and Jan de Witt) whose writings were presented by van Schooten in his edition of Descartes' *Geometria* (see catalogue number 31), Newton gradually mastered the analysis of curved lines, surfaces, and solids. He learned how to use the method of infinite series and extended it by discovering how to expand equations with fractional indices. Most significantly, he developed an approach to the measurement of curved lines that mapped the motion that produced them. This arose out of dissatisfaction with the method of infinitesimals and the advances towards describing curves through their tangents that Newton had so far made. By autumn 1665, Newton had worked out a method for replacing the use of infinitesimal increments of space in his calculations with instantaneous changes in the velocity of a moving point by which curved lines were described. Stimulated entirely by his reading, Newton had invented the method of fluxions, or calculus, through the working in his 'Waste Book'.

Newton was at this stage completely unknown. Others were groping for the solutions that he had found, and, encouraged by Barrow and

Collins, Newton both worked up his own methods and began to think of publishing them. By 1672, he began to have doubts about the wisdom of doing so. Later, the dated evidence of the work in the 'Waste Book' would provide Newton with many of the arguments that he used to assert his priority in discovering the calculus. In October 1676, Newton recorded in the 'Waste Book' the anagrams that concealed his methods for dealing with infinite series (see catalogue number 39). These had been used in letters that he sent to Leibniz about his discoveries. Judging from copies in the Macclesfield Collection, it seems likely that at least one of Newton's champions in the controversy that later broke out with Leibniz, William Jones, had the opportunity to check the chronology of the calculus against the manuscript itself. The 'Waste Book' was not retired by Newton after his initial mathematical labours. He continued to use it extensively for calculations and rough working on the topics that concerned him most. Thus, in the1680s or perhaps even the 1690s, he set down information about the motion of comets in this manuscript.

D.T. Whiteside (ed.), *The Mathematical Papers of Isaac Newton*, 8 vols (Cambridge, 1967–81), vol. 1, especially pp. 145–54; Richard S. Westfall, *Never at Rest. A Biography of Isaac Newton* (Cambridge, 1980), pp. 105–39; Cambridge University Library, Macclesfield Collection, Box 3/4/117–18.

Examined by Thomas Pellet on behalf of Newton's executors, September 1727; presented to Cambridge University Library by the fifth Earl of Portsmouth. See *A Catalogue of the Portsmouth Collection of Books and Papers written by or belonging to Sir Isaac Newton* (Cambridge, 1888), p. 48. One leaf that had been removed from the 'Waste Book' (f. 87) is now in the Macclesfield Collection, Box 43.

34 *Philosophical Transactions*, NUMBER 224 (JANUARY 1697) *(figure 22)*

4°: 3h², 3I-M⁴, 3N²
16.6 × 10 cm
Cambridge University Library, shelfmark T.340.1 b.85.13.

Newton once told his successor as Lucasian Professor, William Whiston, that 'no old Men… love Mathematicks'. After his move to London in 1696, Newton did relax the hectic pace of his mathematical and philosophical activity. Since 1684, he had embarked on a period of concentrated study and calculation that almost rivalled the intensity and brilliance of his work from 1664 to 1675. In addition to the composition and publication of the first edition of the *Principia*, Newton had effectively completed a draft of the *Opticks*. He had taken substantial strides towards the writing of a highly ambitious history of religion and of the spread of idolatry in the Church, and had started to recast much of the *Principia* for a second edition. According to the plans of the early 1690s (see catalogue number 56), this would have made explicit the relationship between the correct understanding of natural philosophy and the true, primitive religion through the restoration of the geometry and wisdom of the ancients. Something certainly deflected Newton from the relentless course that he was following. Perhaps it was age, or a depressing realisation of the difficulty of some the tasks that he had set himself, in searching for solutions that had evaded him as a young man. More probably, changes in his personal circumstances and in public life as a whole forced Newton to lessen his scholarly commitment and withdraw to some extent from the full expression of his most controversial ideas. Newton and his closest allies were far more powerful by the mid-1690s than they had been in the 1680s, but they were also busier and had to bear greater burdens of responsibility. Newton in particular had increasingly more to lose than to gain, especially from any deeper public association with religious controversy at a time of widespread and vicious political and theological disagreement.

Nevertheless, Newton continued to relish the challenge of mathematics, particularly when it was allied to the opportunity to demonstrate his mastery of techniques that others were only beginning to understand. During the 1680s, Gottfried Wilhelm Leibniz, the philosopher to the court of Hanover, had published the first works to make use of new methods of analysis, the differential and integral calculus. By the 1690s, Johann Bernoulli, who became Professor of Mathematics at the University of Groningen in 1695, and several other Continental mathematicians had also mastered the skills necessary to work competently with infinite series and infinitesimals. These developments certainly perturbed Newton, who was later convinced that Leibniz must have taken his inspiration from some of his own, much earlier work. Newton's ideas had initially been communicated to Leibniz through Collins and Oldenburg in 1673. Newton sent Leibniz two detailed accounts in 1676 (see catalogue number 33), in which, despite the occasional use of code, he was remarkably frank about his mathematical knowledge and its development. This correspondence had been

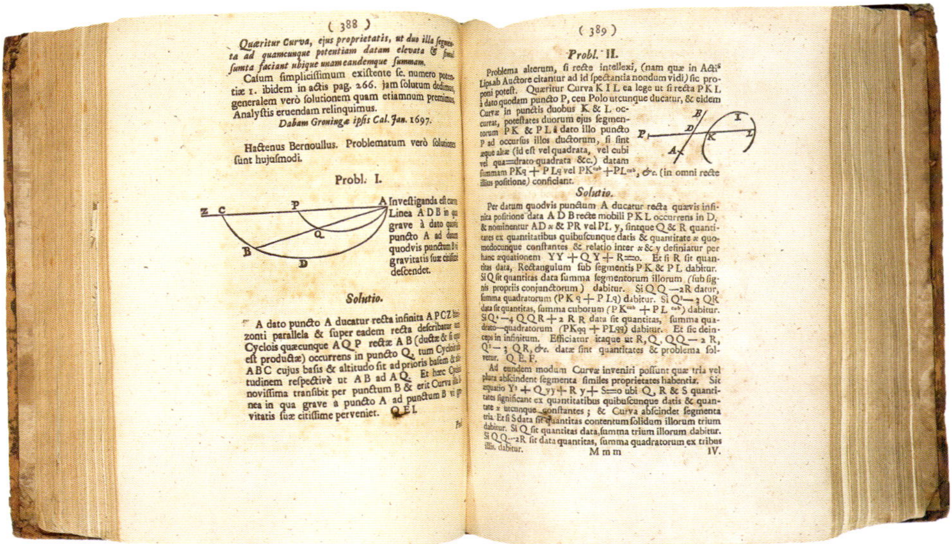

FIGURE 22
Newton's solution to Bernoulli's problem, University Library, T.340.1 b.85.13, pp. 388–9.

interrupted, partly as the result of the death of Oldenburg, in a manner that seemed, with hindsight, to show disrespect on Leibniz's part. Newton's command of infinitesimals was apparent to the few mathematicians who were equipped to recognise it in some of the reasoning of the *Principia*. During the early 1690s, references to Newton's methods also began to appear in some of Wallis' publications. Then, on New Year's Day 1697, Bernoulli issued a proclamation 'to the sharpest mathematicians in the whole world'.

Bernoulli's proclamation represented a challenge to solve two problems relating to curved lines. The first, and subsequently most famous, of these was to determine the shortest path between two given points in a vertical plane taken by a body moving under its own gravity and descending between them in the shortest time. Bernoulli had originally published this problem of the brachistochrone curve in the journal, *Acta eruditorum*, in June 1696. Only Leibniz had sent in a solution within the six-month period then specified for the competition by Bernoulli. The fresh proclamation extended the deadline, in addition adding a second problem to find a curve such that the sum of the segments of a line drawn at random from a fixed pole to cut it at two points is a constant, and threw a gauntlet firmly at Newton's feet. It was directed at 'the very mathematicians who pride themselves that, by the unparalleled methods that they recommend with so much effort, they have not only penetrated most intimately the hiding-places of a more secret Geometry, but have even extended its limits in a remarkable way by their golden theorems which, as they used to think, were known to no-one, but which others had already published a long time before.'

Although both Bernoulli and Leibniz believed that Newton had read the initial announcement of the brachistochrone problem in the *Acta eruditorum*, Newton steadfastly maintained that he was ignorant of its original formulation. According to the solution that he sent to his patron, Charles Montague, on 30 January 1697, the day before the expiry of the time limit for the extended task of Bernoulli's proclamation, Newton had known of the challenge for less than twenty-four hours. His friends later embroidered this fact by suggesting that Newton had received Bernoulli's paper at four in the afternoon, after his day's work at the Mint, and had solved it by four in the morning. Whatever the truth of Newton's acquaintance with Bernoulli's two problems, the character of his solutions left little doubt about the identity of their author when they were published anonymously in the *Philosophical Transactions* (pp. 388–9, on display). They proved conclusively that Newton had indeed penetrated more closely into the lair of the calculus than those who had appeared to mock him. In both of his answers to Bernoulli's examination, Newton had produced more lucid and wide-ranging proofs than those offered either by his tormentor or by any other contemporary mathematician. Bernoulli claimed that he knew immediately who had composed the solutions, remarking later that they gave away Newton's authorship in the same way that a lion was revealed by his claw (or, in a freer translation of Bernoulli's Latin, his footprint).

Newton later provided a simplified solution of the brachistochrone problem (Ms. Add. 3968(41), f. 2r) in response to a lengthy published description by Nicolas Fatio de Duillier. Fatio's essay, which appeared in 1699, kindled the dispute between Newton and Leibniz by suggesting that Newton's unpublished papers would make it clear that he alone had invented the calculus.

D.T. Whiteside (ed.), *The Mathematical Papers of Isaac Newton*, 8 vols (Cambridge, 1967–81), vol. 8, 72–91; H. W. Turnbull, J.F. Scott, A.R. Hall and Laura Tilling (eds), *The Correspondence of Isaac Newton*, 7 vols (Cambridge, 1959–77), vol. 4, 220–9 (where the translations are unfortunately inadequate); William Whiston, *Memoirs*, 2 vols (London, 1749), vol. 1, pp. 315–16; J.A. van Maanen (ed.), *Een complexe grootheid: leven en werk van Johann Bernoulli, 1667–1748* (Utrecht, 1995), pp. 69–92.

35 CAMBRIDGE UNIVERSITY LIBRARY, MS. ADD. 3968, f. 126r
29.8 × 18.8 cm

The dispute about priority in the invention of the calculus smouldered throughout the first decade of the eighteenth century. It caught fire when one of Newton's supporters, the Oxford mathematician John Keill, hinted broadly that Leibniz had plagiarised Newton's work when he had described the calculus for the first time in print. In 1711, Leibniz complained about the accusations of Fatio and Keill in a letter to the secretary of the Royal Society, of which Newton was now President (see catalogue number 40). By then, Newton had begun to allow his disciples access to the manuscripts from his youth that would largely prove his claim to have invented the method (although not the form) of the calculus used by Leibniz. Displaying deviousness in controversy that presented a stark contrast to his relative openness in the 1670s, Newton searched his own records to select passages that seemed to support his case.

Superficially, one of the most telling examples of Newton's priority in the manipulation of infinite series was a tract, entitled 'De analysi per aequationes infinitas' (see catalogue number 36), that Barrow had communicated to Collins on 31 July 1669. Collins had copied the manuscript and then returned the work to Newton. The manuscript on display contains extracts that Newton himself made 'Out of Mr Newton's Treatise de Analysi per aequationes infinitas, ~~communicated~~ sent by Dr Barrow to Mr Collins [the] 31th of July 1669'. It was probably written in 1712, the year in which the Royal Society prepared its response to Leibniz's complaints about the conduct of Keill. Newton presented the initial selections from his papers to the Society on 24 April 1712, at a meeting that endorsed his claims. For much of the rest of the year, in between attempts to solve queries posed by the young editor of the long-awaited second edition of the *Principia* (see catalogue number 60), Newton completed the hunt for evidence and himself drafted the judgement of the Royal Society. This was published in January 1713 with the title *Commercium Epistolicum*; it was almost entirely the work of the man it claimed to vindicate.

D.T. Whiteside (ed.), *The Mathematical Papers of Isaac Newton*, 8 vols (Cambridge, 1967–81), vol. 8, 469–560.

Presented to Cambridge University Library by the fifth Earl of Portsmouth. See *A Catalogue of the Portsmouth Collection of Books and Papers written by or belonging to Sir Isaac Newton* (Cambridge, 1888), pp. 6–8.

36 ISAAC NEWTON, *Analysis per quantitatum series, fluxiones, ac differentias*, ED. WILLIAM JONES

(London, 1711)
4°: π^2, a-c^2, A-Z^2, χ^4, 2a^2, 2B^4
19 × 12.5 cm
Trinity College, Cambridge, shelfmark NQ 8/26

William Jones had already published an edition of the text of 'De analysi' by the time of Newton's work to prepare extracts for submission to the Royal Society (see catalogue number 10). He was also nominally one of the editors appointed by the Royal Society to supervise the compilation of the *Commercium Epistolicum*. In 1708, he had obtained the papers of John Collins, including the original correspondence in which Barrow had discussed Newton's mathematical work for the first time outside Cambridge. Also among Collins' manuscripts were copies that had been made of a number of unpublished papers. One of these was an anonymous version of 'De analysi'. From the correspondence now in his possession, Jones was quickly able to identify Newton as the author of this essay and he began to make preparations for its publication.

Jones was perhaps fortunate in the moment of his acquisition of Collins' archive. It is hard to imagine Newton wishing to collaborate on an edition of his juvenilia at any time before the middle of the first decade of the eighteenth century. Then, however, it started to become increasingly important to him to find clearly dated evidence of his work on infinitesimals during the 1660s. Only by doing this could he establish a significant interval between the moment of his own invention of the calculus and Leibniz's discoveries. The prospect of access to the letters in which he had first described his mathematical activities must have seemed like a godsend. In particular, the correspondence with Collins about Newton's planned additions to Mercator's translation of Kinckhuysen (see catalogue number 27) indicated that he had already reached beyond the mathematical competence of his Continental counterparts. Letters from Barrow and Collins testified to the extent of Newton's abilities even before he had read Mercator's *Logarithmotechnia* (1668), a book that had considerably extended contemporary knowledge of infinite series. It was true that Newton's youthful letters expressed modesty and reservations about the nature of his own discoveries at this point. But the slightly later tract, 'De analysi', which Newton had planned to revise for publication in the early 1670s, suggested a more confident claim to the originality of his thinking. Moreover, as Newton almost certainly realised, Collins had allowed Leibniz sight of his copy of the manuscript when the young German natural philosopher visited London in October 1676.

Newton communicated the autograph copy of 'De analysi' to Jones for use in the preparation of his edition. He also gave permission for Jones to include two other early mathematical papers, 'Enumeratio linearum tertii ordines' and 'Methodus differentialis' in his work. These dated in origin from the late 1660s and early 1670s, as notes in Newton's 'Waste Book' and elsewhere indicate. They bore signs, however, of much more recent revision. This was even more true of the fourth essay that Jones edited, 'De quadratura curvarum', in which Newton's full mastery of the dynamic nature of his calculus and of the peculiar notation that expressed it was made clear (see catalogue number 40). Newton composed this work in the early 1690s, not in the 1660s, as he had hinted when he had published it as an appendix to the *Opticks* in 1704. The pages on display (pp. 42–3), from Newton's copy of Jones' edition, indicate that he was still making changes to the wording of the text after its republication in 1711.

In his introduction to the edition, Jones quoted extensively from the correspondence that he had collected to prove Newton's priority in the invention of the calculus. In about 1712, he placed many of the originals at Newton's disposal. Some of these, together with both Collins' copy and the autograph of 'De analysi', Newton later deposited in the Royal Society. Most of the earliest letters, however, entered the Macclesfield Collection. As a result of his efforts, Jones was elected a Fellow of the Royal Society in 1712. His pride in the blow that he had struck for Newton's cause can be seen in the careful translation that he made of a letter from Charles Réné Reyneau, written in Paris on 23 November 1714: 'I have observ'd with a deal of pleasure, in this Collection, the first discoveries which the Author made, that serv'd to lead him into others, and how he carried them to the utmost perfection'.

D.T. Whiteside (ed.), *The Mathematical Papers of Isaac Newton*, 8 vols (Cambridge, 1967–81), vol. 2, 206–59; vol. 3, 3–19, vol. 7, 3–182; A. Rupert Hall, *Philosophers at War. The Quarrel between Newton and Leibniz* (Cambridge, 1980); Stephen Jordan Rigaud (ed.), *Correspondence of Scientific Men of the Seventeenth Century*, 2 vols (Oxford, 1841; reprinted Hildesheim, 1965); John Harrison, *The Library of Isaac Newton* (Cambridge, 1978), p. 200; Macclesfield Collection, Box 3/4/1.

Listed by the booksellers who appraised Newton's library for his executors; bought with the rest of the library by John Huggins in 1727. Bookplate of Charles Huggins. Bookplate of James Musgrave, with shelfmark E6–32. Presented to Trinity College, Cambridge, on 30 October 1943 by the Pilgrim Trust.

37 CAMBRIDGE UNIVERSITY LIBRARY, MACCLESFIELD COLLECTION, BOX 3/3/91
20.7 × 16.1 cm

Jones' edition also won him praise nearer home. Roger Cotes (1682–1716), who at the time was helping Newton to prepare the second edition of the *Principia* (see catalogue number 60) for the press in Cambridge, wrote on 15 February 1711 to congratulate him on his work. Cotes was well aware of the significance of the 'papers of Sr Isaac's in your hands which were long ago communicated to Mr Collins'. Indeed, he had already advised another potential ally of Newton, Joseph Raphson, to ask Jones if he could make use of them in the history of the calculus on which he had been working.

By February 1711, Cotes had been assisting Newton with the editing of the second edition of the *Principia* for about two years. The initial flood of material that Newton had sent to Cotes had slowed to a trickle. As Cotes pointed out to Jones: 'We are now at a stand as to Sr Isaac's Principia; he designs to make some few Experiments before we proceed any further. The first Book & [the] six first sections of [the] second are printed off.' Cotes was being typically tactful in these remarks. The delay with Book II of the *Principia* was largely a product of revisions that Cotes had persuaded Newton to undertake in order to correct errors and obscurities that he had found in the text. These and other corrections and additions held up the delivery of the final copy for the second edition of the *Principia* for a further two years. Cotes himself composed the preface for the book, in which he controversially set out the importance of the Newtonian understanding of gravity for natural philosophy.

H. W. Turnbull, J.F. Scott, A.R. Hall and Laura Tilling (eds), *The Correspondence of Isaac Newton*, 7 vols (Cambridge, 1959–77), vol. 5, 94–5 (which prints this letter).

Purchased from the Earl of Macclesfield by Cambridge University Library, August 2000.

38 CAMBRIDGE UNIVERSITY LIBRARY, MS. ADD. 3977(9), ff. 1v-2r *(figure 23)* 23.1 × 17.9 cm

This letter, dated 5 July 1671, is one of many that John Collins (1625–83) exchanged with the young Isaac Newton. After a three-year apprenticeship to an Oxford bookseller, Collins had spent seven years as a sailor in the Mediterranean, mostly in Venetian service. Returning to London, he earned a living as a mathematical teacher in the 1650s, and published a number of practical works. By summer 1669, when Isaac Barrow prompted him to open a correspondence with Newton, Collins had been working as a clerk in the civil service for nearly ten years. The main passion of his life, however, was the exchange of mathematical information. His skill at letter writing and knowledge of the printing trade provided invaluable assistance to Oldenburg in sustaining the work of the Royal Society, of which Collins became a fellow in 1667. He was also instrumental in encouraging a number of younger mathematical authors, both English and foreign, to put their ideas into print.

Newton was one of the authors whom Collins encouraged (see catalogue number 36), circulating news of his ideas to the Scottish mathematician James Gregory and others, pressing the bookseller Moses Pitt to publish his work in the form of additions to Kinckhuysen's introduction to algebra, and generally providing him with a window on the wider world of British and European mathematics. In return, the young Newton trusted Collins with his mathematical discoveries, particularly with the text of 'De analysi' and his work on infinite series. As the draft of his reply to this letter indicates, Newton was almost embarrassed by Collins' generosity in sending him books. He was also candid about his progress. He marked with a cross two passages in Collins' letter. These asked him about Kinckhuysen's introduction and warned him not 'to overhasten the publication of your thoughts for being prevented by

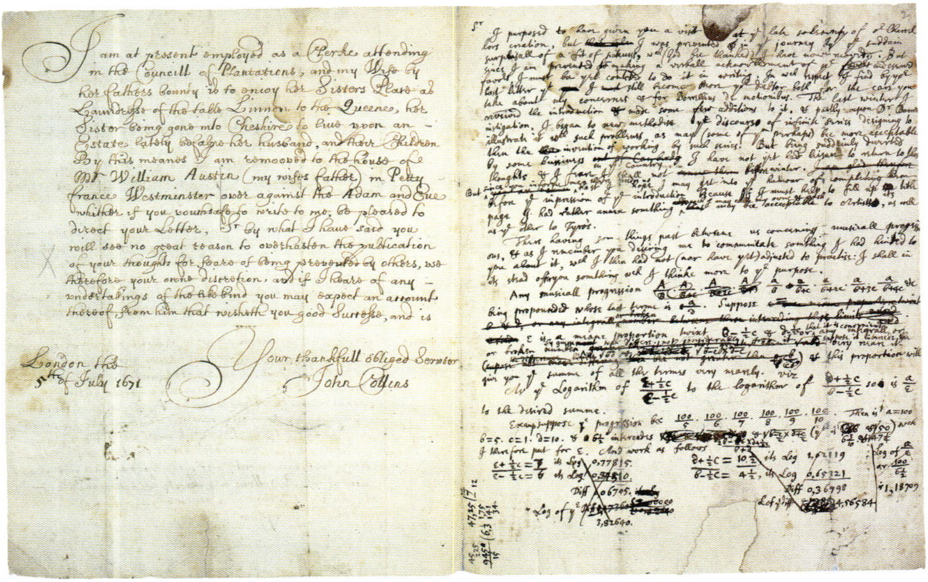
I am at present employed as a Clerke attending in the Councell of Plantations, and my Wife by her fathers Bounty is to enjoy her Sisters Place as Laundresse of the table Linnen to the Queenes, her Sister being gone into Cheshire to live upon an Estate lately left her husband, and their Children By this meanes I am removed to the house of Mr William Austin (my wifes father) in Petty france Westminster over against the Adam and Eve whither if you vouchsafe to write to me, be pleased to direct your Letter, Sr by what I have said you will see no great reason to overhasten the publication of your thoughts for feare of being prevented by others, use therefore your owne discretion, and if I heare of any undertakings of the like kind you may expect an account thereof from him that wisheth you good Successe, and is

London the 5th of July 1671

Your thankfull obliged Servitor
John Collins

FIGURE 23
A letter from John Collins to Newton, with a draft of Newton's reply. Letters like this later helped Newton to establish the chronology of his discoveries and to claim priority in the invention of the calculus, University Library, Ms. Add. 3977(9), ff. 1v-2r.

others'. Newton's reply was full and displayed a relish for the prospect of appearing in print that he would soon regret:'The last winter I reveiwed the introduction & made some few additions to it, & partly upon Dr Barrow['s] instigation, I began to new methodise [that] discourse of infinite series'.

This openness would later come to Newton's aid, once Collins' papers had passed into William Jones' hands. It was relatively unusual for Newton to preserve drafts of his letters. Collins, however, kept the correspondence that he received with the same care with which he collected or copied documents that related to the history of seventeenth-century mathematics. Thus, for example, the reply that Newton drafted here and sent on 20 July 1671 can now be found in the Macclesfield Collection.

H. W. Turnbull, J.F. Scott, A.R. Hall and Laura Tilling (eds), *The Correspondence of Isaac Newton*, 7 vols (Cambridge, 1959–77), vol. 1, 65–71 (printing both letter and reply).

Presented to Cambridge University Library by the fifth Earl of Portsmouth. See *A Catalogue of the Portsmouth Collection of Books and Papers written by or belonging to Sir Isaac Newton* (Cambridge, 1888), pp. 32–3.

39 CAMBRIDGE UNIVERSITY LIBRARY, MACCLESFIELD COLLECTION, BOX 3/4/56
29.8 × 18.5 cm

On 24 October 1676, Newton wrote to Henry Oldenburg, sending a reply to a letter from Leibniz whose contents Oldenburg had communicated to him. Leibniz had just left London, where he had visited Collins and other natural philosophers. The reply to Leibniz that Newton enclosed was more guarded than an earlier letter written in June 1676. It again praised Leibniz's work with infinite series and gave a detailed and comparatively modest account of the history and scope of Newton's own discoveries (see catalogue number 34). It was also generous in its recognition of the work of earlier mathematicians. Nevertheless, Newton was careful to conceal some of his more advanced discoveries, notably his own version of the calculus (the method of fluxions), by means of two insoluble anagrams (see catalogue number 33). Although Newton soon worried that he had been too severe, he also cautioned Oldenburg on 26 October: 'let none of my mathematical papers be printed [without] my special licence' and expressed reluctance about being drawn into any further mathematical communication. Misunderstandings of Leibniz's behaviour later convinced Newton that both he and his friends had been far too incautious in this correspondence.

H. W. Turnbull, J.F. Scott, A.R. Hall and Laura Tilling (eds), *The Correspondence of Isaac Newton*, 7 vols (Cambridge, 1959–77), vol. 2, 109–63 (which prints this letter and the enclosure for Leibniz).

Purchased from the Earl of Macclesfield by Cambridge University Library, August 2000.

40 CAMBRIDGE UNIVERSITY LIBRARY, MS. ADD. 3968, f. 262r
32.8 × 20.9

Leibniz learned of John Keill's attack on his calculus early in 1711. On 4 March (21 February in England) 1711, he complained to Hans Sloane, the secretary of the Royal Society, in whose *Philosophical Transactions* Keill's work had appeared. Leibniz bemoaned 'this most impertinent accusation', which suggested that his calculus was merely Newton's method of fluxions in disguise. Although he did not accuse Keill directly of malice, he argued that he was nevertheless owed a public apology, which the Royal Society should secure. Sloane, who did not always see eye to eye with Newton, copied Leibniz's letter and dispatched it to the President of the Royal Society himself. There the matter rested for a month. Keill read parts of his reply to Leibniz at the Royal Society on 22 March, and subsequently sent Newton the reference to a review of 'De quadratura curvarum' (see catalogue number 36) that had been published anonymously in the *Acta eruditorum* in 1705. This seemed to suggest that Newton had depended on Leibniz's calculus when writing the *Principia*. Leibniz was clearly the review's author. He was no doubt responding to the suggestion that Fatio had made that Newton was the only inventor of the calculus, as well as to Newton's own attempts to pass off his mature work as juvenilia. But once the review was known in England, Newton set out mercilessly and deliberately to prove Leibniz wrong.

H. W. Turnbull, J.F. Scott, A.R. Hall and Laura Tilling (eds), *The Correspondence of Isaac Newton*, 7 vols (Cambridge, 1959–77), vol. 5, 96–8 (which prints this letter), 115–18, 132–52.

Presented to Cambridge University Library by the fifth Earl of Portsmouth. See *A Catalogue of the Portsmouth Collection of Books and Papers written by or belonging to Sir Isaac Newton* (Cambridge, 1888), pp. 6–8.

41 CAMBRIDGE UNIVERSITY LIBRARY, MS. ADD. 3968, f. 67r
30.2 × 18.5 cm

The publication of the *Commercium epistolicum* in 1713 did little to resolve the dispute between Newton and Leibniz. With the aid of Bernoulli, Leibniz replied mockingly to Newton's legalistic attempt to demonstrate mathematical priority through the dates of letters and the publication of manuscripts that contained only elements of the mature calculus. Newton set to work in turn on 'An Account of the Commercium Epistolicum', an anonymous review of the evidence that was published in the *Philosophical Transactions* in January/February 1715. Here, he rehearsed the testimony provided by 'ancient letters & Papers'.

By the time of his death in 1716, Leibniz was at war with Newton on a number of fronts. The controversy over the calculus showed no sign of resolution. Criticisms of Newton's natural philosophy had been given new life by the publication of the queries to the *Opticks* (see catalogue numbers 29 and 30) and by the General Scholium and Cotes' preface to the second edition of the *Principia* (see catalogue number 60). Leibniz raised doubts in particular about Newton's explanations for the role of gravity, suggesting that his arguments were both philosophically and theologically unsound. It seemed likely that he would convince his patron, Caroline of Ansbach, who had become Princess of Wales on the death of Queen Anne in 1714. Yet, despite the widespread success of Leibniz's supporters on the Continent, Newton and his allies won both the battle of ideas and the battle for patronage in England. They did so at a cost, however. The myth of Newton's youthful brilliance went hand in hand with resentment towards an often cantankerous and autocratic old man. Many of those who were cowed by the calculus, which they did not understand, nevertheless remained sceptical about Newton's metaphysical speculations that seemed to smack of a heretical theology.

D.T. Whiteside (ed.), *The Mathematical Papers of Isaac Newton*, 8 vols (Cambridge, 1967–81), vol. 8, 469–624.

PHILOSOPHIÆ NATURALIS PRINCIPIA MATHEMATICA.

Autore *JS. NEWTON*, *Trin. Coll. Cantab. Soc.* Matheseos Professore *Lucasiano*, & Societatis Regalis Sodali.

IMPRIMATUR.
S. PEPYS, *Reg. Soc.* PRÆSES.
Julii 5. 1686.

LONDINI,

Jussu *Societatis Regiæ* ac Typis *Josephi Streater*. Prostat apud plures Bibliopolas. *Anno* MDCLXXXVII.

GLORY AND GRAVITY

FIGURE 24
Title-page of the first edition of the *Principia* (1687), from a copy that belonged to the Lancastrian astronomer and natural philosopher, Richard Towneley (1629–1707), University Library, Adams 5.68.3.

The publication of the *Principia* in 1687 secured Newton's intellectual reputation. It was the culmination of almost three years of frantic effort by Newton and by Edmond Halley, who saw the book through the press in London. Although many of the ideas in the *Principia* can be traced back as far as the 1660s, the form in which they were set out and the conclusions that were drawn from them were very much the product of the years 1684–7. In August 1684, Halley told Newton about a conversation that he had had at the Royal Society concerning planetary motion. Anxious that others might take the credit for discoveries that he felt were already his, Newton went to work to prove his theories of celestial dynamics. Drafts were composed and rushed to Halley in London to indicate Newton's priority. Copies of some of them were later deposited in the University Library as if they had been his Lucasian lectures. Yet, despite the haste, these manuscripts show that Newton had indeed now solved the principal problems of celestial mechanics. The final text of the *Principia* set out his mature thoughts about the operation (although not the cause) of gravity. Structured to follow the rules of scientific reasoning that Newton developed, the *Principia* nevertheless baffled many readers, who complained that not even its author could possibly understand it.

42 KING'S COLLEGE, CAMBRIDGE, KEYNES MS. 97, NUMBER 1
30.1 × 18.5

If, in midsummer 1684, Newton had any plans for the publication of a work of mathematics or natural philosophy, his attention was probably focussed on one of two possible subjects. The first of these was the treatment of the geometry of curved lines, on which he had recently been working; the second concerned his discoveries in the manipulation of infinite series and the invention of the calculus. Some of the ideas that

Newton long ago communicated to Collins had begun to surface in public. In particular, David Gregory, then a young professor of mathematics in Edinburgh, had recently published work that drew on knowledge of Newton's techniques. Gregory derived his information from his uncle, James, also a noted mathematician and natural philosopher. James Gregory, in turn, had been a consistent correspondent of Collins, who had first mentioned Newton to him in 1669.

By autumn 1684, however, Newton's attention was concentrated elsewhere, in an attempt to prove that the planets move in elliptical orbits as a result of the constant action of a force inversely proportional to the square of their distance from the sun. This sudden change of emphasis had been provoked by a visit from Edmond Halley (1656–1742), which probably took place in August. Halley may have met Newton in 1682, shortly after he returned to England from a journey through France and Italy. Halley's account of making the earliest evening observation of the comet of 1680 on the road to Paris certainly found its way into Newton's 'Waste Book' (see catalogue number 33) around this time. Halley had been elected to the Council of the Royal Society in 1683, and, when he called on Newton, he told him about a conversation that he had had with Robert Hooke and Sir Christopher Wren at a meeting of the Society on 14 January 1684. Hooke had claimed to be able to demonstrate that an inverse square law governed celestial mechanics. In response to this boast, Wren had set a challenge by offering a prize to the first of his companions who could prove the operation of this law.

Newton had been interested in the motion of heavenly bodies since the mid-1660s (see catalogue number 2). The idea of the inverse square law was in many ways a natural development of Johannes Kepler's laws of planetary motion, by then quite well known in England, in the light of Cartesian thinking about the force possessed by a body in motion. Descartes' influence was certainly apparent in the papers on motion that Newton composed in the late 1660s and early 1670s. In one of these, Newton had invoked Kepler's third law and extrapolated from it to an inverse square law applying to the 'endeavour [conatus] in the principal planets of receding from the sun'. He subsequently told both Halley and David Gregory that he had composed these words in 1673, before the publication of Christiaan Huygens' thoughts on the subject. Wren had discussed the possible operation of an inverse square law with Newton in 1677 and Hooke had touched on it in an exchange of letters with Newton between November 1679 and January 1680. Hooke had initiated this correspondence on becoming Secretary of the Royal Society, in an effort to tempt Newton out of the self-imposed silence into which he had retreated after 1676. Despite this, his delight in making mischief was so great, or his need for information so desperate, that he rushed to announce trials at the Royal Society of Newton's erroneous proposal that the path of a body falling towards the rotating earth might be a spiral. After nearly a year of total silence, Newton acknowledged Hooke's correction in the curtest possible manner. Nevertheless, it later appeared that Hooke's prompting played a significant role in encouraging Newton once more to think seriously about the behaviour of bodies moving under gravity.

Thus, when Halley told him about Hooke's boasting in 1684, Newton was able to claim that he could now provide the necessary proof that an inverse square law governed the motion of the planets. Unfortunately, it turned out that he was unable to find where he had written this proof down. Nevertheless, by November, Newton had sent Halley a new tract, 'De motu', in which he had already extended his earlier thoughts. Newton realised that not just the planets but all heavenly bodies were governed by the same principles of force. Moreover, he had introduced for the first time an absolute notion of force, as distinct from the Cartesian notion that force might be relative to the body being moved. Despite the excitement that 'De motu' generated at the Royal Society, it was only a beginning. For the next year and a half, Newton worked furiously to clarify his definitions and to extend his calculations to heavenly bodies other than planets. Here, the observations of a comet that he had made in 1664 (see catalogue number 2) were put to work alongside the more detailed information that he had amassed about the comet of 1680 (see catalogue numbers 44 and 48). So intense was Newton's absorption in this new project (see catalogue numbers 7 and 16) that he seems to have abandoned his other activities entirely, breaking off the record of some chemical experiments in May 1684 and only picking it up again in April 1686 (see catalogue numbers 11 and 14).

On 28 April 1686, the Royal Society received the text of Book I of the *Principia*. Despite the prolonged absence of many members of its Council, the Society decided on 19 May that it should publish Newton's work. Halley, who was now the Society's Clerk, was 'intrusted to look after the printing it'. He immediately wrote to Newton on 22 May (letter on display) to consult him about publication and to warn him that Hooke had 'some pretension upon the invention of [the] rule of the decrease of Gravity, being reciprocally as the squares of the distances from the Center. He sais you had the notion from him, though he owns the Demonstration of the Curves generated thereby to be wholly your own…' Newton's reply dismissed Hooke's claims and he welcomed the first proofs that Halley sent him in June. But the prospect of bitter controversy made Newton anxious about some of what he had written. On 20 June he wrote to promise Halley the text of Book II of the *Principia*, which he had finished the previous summer, but warned 'I designed [the] whole to consist of three books… The third wants [the] Theory of Comets. In Autumn last I spent two months in calculations to no purpose for want of a good method, [which] made me afterwards return to [the] first Book & enlarge it [with] divers Propositions… The third I now designe to suppress.' He continued: 'Philosophy is such an impertinently litigious Lady that a man had as good be engaged in Law suits as have to with her. I found it so formerly & now I no sooner come near her again but she gives me warning.'

The final form of the *Principia* owed much to Halley's tact and patience. He encouraged Newton to persevere with Book III and waited quietly for its arrival. He supervised the printer and designed the woodcuts to illustrate the text. He tolerated Newton's further delays, agreeing to his desire that the completion of the book be postponed until at least late spring 1687. Above all, Halley accepted the costs of the publication of the book himself. The Royal Society was at the time as good as bankrupt, reduced to paying its officers, including Halley, in unsold copies of the lavish *History of Fishes* that it had published in 1686. Moreover, Halley's position had come under threat at the Society's elections, perhaps as a result of lobbying by Hooke.

I. Bernard Cohen, *Introduction to Newton's 'Principia'* (Cambridge, 1971), pp. 47–81; H. W. Turnbull, J.F. Scott, A.R. Hall and Laura Tilling (eds), *The Correspondence of Isaac Newton*, 7 vols (Cambridge, 1959–77), vol. 1, 297–303; vol. 2, 297–314, 400–402, 431–66 (part of which prints this letter); D.T. Whiteside (ed.), *The Mathematical Papers of Isaac Newton*, 8 vols (Cambridge, 1967–81), vol. 4, 409–653; Richard S. Westfall, *Never at Rest. A Biography of Isaac Newton* (Cambridge, 1980), pp. 378–90, 402–68; A. Rupert Hall and Marie Boas Hall (eds), *Unpublished Scientific Papers of Isaac Newton* (Cambridge, 1962), pp. 157–64, 231–301; John Herivel, *The Background to Newton's Principia* (Oxford, 1965); A. Rupert Hall, 'Newton on the Calculation of Central Forces', *Annals of Science*, 13 (1957), 62–71;

Thomas Birch (ed.), *The History of the Royal Society of London*, 4 vols (London, 1756–7), vol. 3, p. 519; vol. 4, 347, 370, 479–80, 486, 491, 527, 545; Alan Cook, *Edmond Halley* (Oxford, 1998), pp. 147–78.

Sotheby sale, 13 July 1936, lot 137; purchased by Gabriel Wells for £310 and subsequently sold to J.M. Keynes. Exhibited 5 July–29 August 1983, Fitzwilliam Museum, Cambridge: David Scrase and Peter Croft, *Maynard Keynes. Collector of Pictures, Books and Manuscripts* (Cambridge, 1983), pp. 83–4.

43 ISAAC NEWTON, *Philosophiae naturalis principia mathematica*

(London, 1687)
(figures 24 & 25)
4°: A-3O⁴
19.7 × 13.4 cm
Cambridge University Library, shelfmark Adv. b. 39.1

On 5 July 1687, Halley wrote to Newton: 'I have at length brought your Book to an end, and hope it will please you. the last errata came just in time to be inserted.' Despite the acclaim that greeted his achievements, however, Newton still felt that there was more to be done. A particular problem remained the explanation of universal gravitation. Newton's treatment of gravity had been one of the revolutionary aspects of his work. By showing that its effects could account in detail for the movements of the heavens, Newton had been able to give universal force to the laws of motion that he propounded. Yet, in the eyes of many of his most distinguished contemporaries, his achievement was qualified by the failure to provide a properly philosophical account of gravity. Newton could describe the effects of gravitation but he could not explain them adequately. Newton's friend, Nicolas Fatio de Duillier, felt that he had the answer and, for a time in the early 1690s, it seemed possible that he might produce a new edition of the *Principia*. Others of Newton's growing band of young disciples, particularly David Gregory, also discussed his plans to augment the work.

Newton himself returned to his chemical experiments (see catalogue number 14) and to the optical papers of the mid-1670s (see catalogue numbers 26 and 28). With Fatio's prompting, he reconsidered the possibility that some sort of subtle matter or aether might be responsible for the effects of gravity. Newton's historical and theological reading encouraged him to search for more wide-ranging philosophical explanations. He confided many of these to Gregory, in particular ideas that the divine will itself might animate the actions of gravity. Newton was by

[402]

REGULÆ PHILOSOPHANDI.

~~HYPOTHESES.~~

Reg. ~~Hypoth.~~ I. *Causas rerum naturalium non plures admitti debere, quàm quæ & vera sint & earum Phænomenis explicandis sufficiant.*

Dicunt utique Philosophi: Natura nihil agit frustra, et frustra fit per plura quod fieri potest per pauciora.

Natura enim simplex est & rerum causis superfluis non luxuriat.

Reg. ~~Hypoth.~~ II. *Ideoque effectuum naturalium ejusdem generis eædem sunt causæ.*

Uti respirationis in Homine & in Bestia; descensûs lapidum in *Europa* & in *America*; Lucis in Igne culinari & in Sole; reflexionis lucis in Terra & in Planetis.

Hypoth. III. *Corpus omne in alterius cujuscunque generis corpus transformari posse, & qualitatum gradus omnes intermedios successivè induere.*

Hypoth. IV. *Centrum Systematis Mundani quiescere.*

Hoc ab omnibus concessum est, dum aliqui Terram alii Solem ~~in centro quiescere contendant.~~

PHÆNOMENA.

Phænom. ~~Hypoth.~~ ~~V~~ I. *Planetas circumjoviales, radiis ad centrum Jovis ductis, areas describere temporibus proportionales, eorumque tempora periodica esse in ratione sesqui~~altera~~plicata distantiarum ab ipsius centro.*

Constat ex observationibus Astronomicis. Orbes horum Planetarum non differunt sensibiliter à circulis Jovi concentricis, & motus eorum in his circulis uniformes deprehenduntur. Tempora verò periodica esse in ratione sesqui~~altera~~plicata semidiametrorum orbium consentiunt Astronomi: & ~~Flamstedius, qui omnia Micrometro & per Eclipses Satellitum accuratius definivit, literis ad me datis, quinetiam numeris suis mecum communicatis, significavit rationem illam sesqui~~alteram~~plicatam tam accuratè obtinere, quàm sit possibile sensu deprehendere. Id quod~~ idem ex Tabula sequente manifestum est.

Satellitum

FIGURE 25
Newton's own copy of the *Principia*, marked with revisions for the second edition, University Library, shelfmark Adv. b. 39.1, p. 402.

now familiar with a wide range of classical and patristic sources, with the ideas of Philo of Alexandria, and with the syncretising interpretations that had been placed on them by early modern authors, including the Cambridge Platonists and, perhaps, Justus Lipsius. He came to believe that these sources provided evidence to support his interpretation of gravity. They allowed him to construct a history of religion in which his own metaphysical speculations became identical with the true doctrinal foundations of pristine belief.

The marriage of theology, ancient history, and philosophy that Newton attempted to broker in the 1690s (see catalogue number 56) in fact looked back to work that he had suppressed in the mid-1680s. This included the drafts that he had initially composed for what became Books II and III of the *Principia*, as well as the related 'Theologiae gentilis origines philosophicae' (see catalogue number 15). In the manuscript of 'De motu corporum liber secundus' (see catalogue number 7), Newton gave an account of the fluid heavens through which both planets and comets were propelled by a force that obeyed the inverse square law. This began with a discussion of the philosophy of the ancient atomists, the religion of Numa Pompilius, and the astronomy of the Egyptians and Babylonians. These were Newton's predecessors in the restoration of the true understanding of nature, who had had privileged access to the teachings of a pristine religion before its corruption by vain men. Increasingly, the writings of Newton and his closest disciples would focus on the restoration of religion that had to follow the rediscovery of ancient philosophy. At the same time, Newton began to collect further evidence that ancient understandings of gravity and of celestial motion were similar to his.

Most of Newton's difficulties continued to relate to the final parts of Book II and to Book III of the *Principia*. At the start of Book III, he had defined a number of hypotheses that would govern his approach to natural phenomena. He began to modify these in the early 1690s, gradually developing them into a set of rules for the practice of natural philosophy. These rules were supposed to underpin the interpretation of a group of phenomena that Newton again introduced in changes that he made to the text of the first edition. Newton entered these corrections onto p. 402 of an interleaved copy of the *Principia* (see figure 25) and onto the blank leaf facing that page. On 21 July 1706, David Gregory wrote: 'Sir Isaac Newton shewed me a copy of his Princ. Math. Phil. Nat.

interleaved, and corrected for the Press. It is intirely finished as farr as Sect. VII. Lib. II. pag. 317. He takes this same Sect. VII. to be the hardest part of the book... In the beginning of Lib. III. he leaves out Hyp. III, and puts another in its place... These three he now calls *Regulae Philosophandi*. Hyp. V. &c he calls by the title of *Phaenomena*. Hyp. IV is the only one that he leaves that name to; & it comes after the *Phaenomena*.'

Preparations for the printing of a second edition of the *Principia* began in 1708. The changes that Gregory had described were eventually incorporated in that edition. A few of Newton's more adventurous ideas of the 1690s also persisted in the form of a new 'General Scholium' at the end of Book III (see catalogue number 62). A fourth 'Regula Philosophandi' was added to the third edition of the *Principia* in 1726. Taken together, such alterations helped to establish the myth of Newton as a philosopher who did not 'feign hypotheses'. Yet, paradoxically, that was exactly how he had originally started to explain the system of the world.

H. W. Turnbull, J.F. Scott, A.R. Hall and Laura Tilling (eds), *The Correspondence of Isaac Newton*, 7 vols (Cambridge, 1959–77), vol. 2, 481–2; Betty Jo Teeter Dobbs, *The Janus Faces of Genius* (Cambridge, 1991), pp. 169–212; Rudolf de Smet and Karin Verelst, 'Newton's Scholium Generale: The Platonic and Stoic Legacy – Philo, Justus Lipsius and the Cambridge Platonists', *History of Science*, 39 (2001), 1–30; Robert Iliffe, '"Is he like other men?" The Meaning of the *Principia Mathematica* and the Author as Idol', in Gerald MacLean (ed.), *Culture and Society in the Stuart Restoration* (Cambridge, 1995), 159–76; I. Bernard Cohen, *Introduction to Newton's 'Principia'* (Cambridge, 1971), pp. 23–6 and plates 2–3; Alexandre Koyré and I. Bernard Cohen (eds), *Isaac Newton's Philosophiae Naturalis Principia Mathematica*, 2 vols (Cambridge, 1972), vol. 2, 550–5; W.G. Hiscock (ed.), *David Gregory, Isaac Newton and their Circle* (Oxford, 1937), pp. 36–7; John Harrison, *The Library of Isaac Newton* (Cambridge, 1978), pp. 22, 202.

Listed as imperfect by the booksellers who appraised Newton's library for his executors [at some point this book was badly damaged by fire and water]; presented to Cambridge University Library by the fifth Earl of Portsmouth. See *A Catalogue of the Portsmouth Collection of Books and Papers written by or belonging to Sir Isaac Newton* (Cambridge, 1888), p. 47.

44 CAMBRIDGE UNIVERSITY LIBRARY, MS. ADD. 3965, f. 355r
29.8 × 18.7 cm

The appearance of a comet in November 1680 (see catalogue number 48) had entranced astronomers across Europe, Newton included. The comet blazed particularly brightly in the morning sky towards the end of the month, before appearing to fall into the sun. Shortly after the end of the first week of December, observers noticed a second, spectacular comet in the evening sky, moving away from the sun. Newton tracked the movements of the new comet, eventually using a seven-foot refracting telescope with micrometer for this purpose. He was able to record its position into early March, later than anyone else. At first, Newton, like almost every other astronomer, believed he had seen two different comets during the winter of 1680–1. The Astronomer Royal, John Flamsteed, who had observed the comet from Greenwich was however sceptical about this. In correspondence with Newton, he suggested that there might only ever have been a single comet. Newton was at first intrigued by Flamsteed's theory that comets reversed their direction near the sun, but he was not convinced. Nevertheless, he continued to collect information about the comet from a variety of acquaintances and to try to tabulate their findings. He observed the comet of 1682 (see catalogue number 47) with interest.

Newton's work in the early years of the 1680s began to convince him that the paths of comets might be conic sections, rather than straight lines. Eventually, in proposition XLI of Book III of the *Principia*, he plotted a parabolic orbit for the comet of 1680–1. In the process, he modified his criticism of Flamsteed. By autumn 1685, he accepted that there had only been one comet in 1680–1. He also adopted a version of Flamsteed's suggestion that some form of magnetism attracted and repelled comets from the sun. Newton, however, did not ascribe the motion of comets to a magnetic force. He argued instead that it was a product of universal gravitation.

Much of Newton's continued work on Book III of the *Principia* was designed to support these claims. This became particularly important for him since he gradually assigned a larger and larger role to comets in his cosmology. The paths of comets undermined Cartesian explanations of celestial mechanics and established the power of Newton's concept of universal gravitation. Ideas about comets also supported the theories about ancient wisdom and philosophy that Newton developed from the mid-1680s. As the second edition of the *Principia* advanced, he came to believe that comets played an essential role in the circulation of active principles that promoted change and motion around the universe. He indicated to his disciples that comets were the means by which God managed his creation, suggesting that they were intimately involved in the key events of human history. Stars and planets themselves might once have been comets, and the collision of a comet with the earth might bring about the final conflagration of the world that Christians expected at the end of days. The techniques that Halley developed to calculate the period of return of comets and hence to plot some of their orbits as ellipses were deployed to support these arguments (see catalogue number 49). Thus by 1714, Newton's successor as Lucasian Professor, William Whiston, had calculated that the passage of the comet of 1680–1 had once been responsible for causing Noah's Flood.

Newton communicated the calculations on display to Roger Cotes in October 1712, as he completed the revisions to Book III for the second edition of the *Principia*. Based on Flamsteed's records (see catalogue number 18) and refined by Halley's techniques, they set out a method for correcting observations of the apparent position of comets when seen from the earth. This procedure allowed Newton to determine accurately the paths of comets through the heavens and provided the information to support his calculation of their parabolic or elliptical orbits. Newton later added calculations for the comet of 1723 to these tables of the comets of 1683 and 1682 in the third edition of the *Principia* (1726).

J.A. Ruffner, 'Newton's Propositions on Comets: Steps in Transition, 1681–84', *Archive for History of Exact Sciences*, 54 (2000), 259–77; Sara Schechner Genuth, *Comets, Popular Culture, and the Birth of Modern Cosmology* (Princeton, 1977), pp. 133–215, 270–306; Simon Schaffer, 'Comets & Idols: Newton's Cosmology and Political Theology', in Paul Theerman and Adele F. Seeff, *Action and Reaction* (Newark, 1993), pp. 206–31; David C. Kubrin, 'Newton and the Cyclical Cosmos: Providence and the Mechanical Philosophy', *Journal of the History of Ideas*, 28 (1967), 325–46; Gary W. Kronk, *Cometography*, vol. 1 (Cambridge, 1999), pp. 369–78; H. W. Turnbull, J.F. Scott, A.R. Hall and Laura Tilling (eds), *The Correspondence of Isaac Newton*, 7 vols (Cambridge, 1959–77), vol. 2, 315–430; vol. 5, 347–8; Betty Jo Teeter Dobbs, *The Janus Faces of Genius* (Cambridge, 1991), pp. 169–212; I. Bernard Cohen, *Introduction to Newton's 'Principia'* (Cambridge, 1971), pp. 235–6; Alexandre Koyré and I. Bernard Cohen (eds), *Isaac Newton's Philosophiae Naturalis Principia Mathematica*, 2 vols (Cambridge, 1972), vol. 2, 748–58.

Presented to Cambridge University Library by the fifth Earl of Portsmouth. See *A Catalogue of the Portsmouth Collection of Books and Papers written by or belonging to Sir Isaac Newton* (Cambridge, 1888), pp. 4–5.

MAKING SENSE OF MOTION

Gravity was one of a number of forces whose operation Newton investigated in his working papers and eventually in the *Principia*. Unfortunately, Newton's description of force generated problems for the explanations of matter in motion that he had once accepted and that continued to be used by many of his contemporaries. One consequence of this was that the search for a material cause for the effects of gravity and other forces was a prominent theme in his writing both before and after the publication of the *Principia*. This was particularly noticeable in the queries that he composed for later editions of the *Opticks*, which eventually seemed to propound some sort of spiritual origin for gravity. Despite such difficulties, his account of gravity was triumphantly successful in its solution to some of the outstanding problems of seventeenth-century science. One of the most notable examples of this success was the proof of the parabolic or elliptical orbits of comets. Based on exhaustive investigation of the historical record, the collection of contemporary observations, and careful calculation, this was a critical example of the accuracy of Newton's interpretation of celestial mechanics.

45 CAMBRIDGE UNIVERSITY LIBRARY, MACCLESFIELD COLLECTION, BOX 3/4/62
(figure 26)
29.3 × 18.3

Newton had first become acquainted with the writings of Robert Boyle (1627–91) in the mid-1660s (see catalogue number 11). The two men met at the Royal Society in 1675. As Newton's work on light progressed in the mid-1670s, he began to depend more and more on notions derived from chemical experiments and from consideration of the form and structure of matter. These were techniques and topics that Boyle had

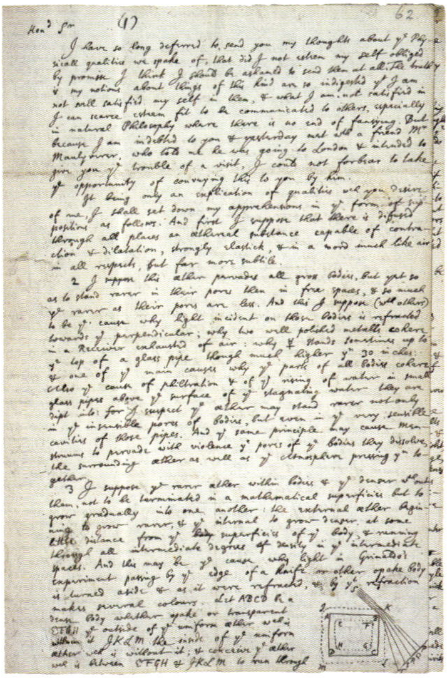

26

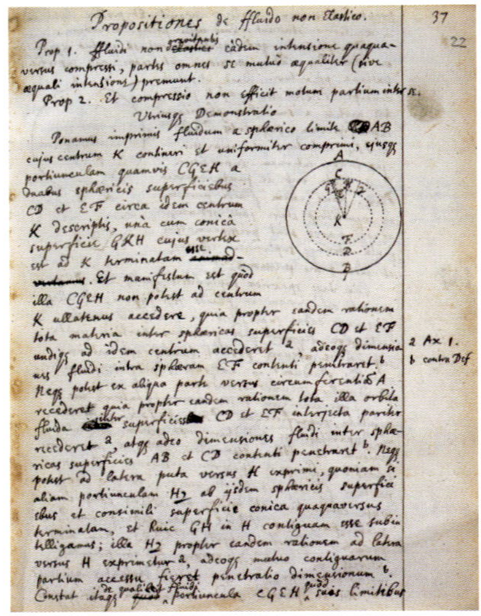

27

FIGURE 26
Newton writes to Boyle about the nature of the aether and the possible mechanical causes of the behaviour of light, University Library, Macclesfield Collection, Box 3/4/62.

FIGURE 27
The effects of gravity in a uniformly contained fluid, from Newton's essay 'De gravitatione et aequipondio fluidorum', University Library, Ms. Add. 4003, f. 22r.

discussed extensively and Newton's notebooks from this period frequently mention both Boyle's own writings and the works that had influenced them. Newton's only surviving letter to Boyle (figure 26) was written on 28 February 1679 and developed ideas that Newton had advanced in earlier correspondence with Oldenburg (see catalogue numbers 26 and 28). In particular, it discussed the nature of the aether, which Newton supposed 'pervades all gross bodies, but yet so as to stand rarer in their pores then in free spaces, & so much [the] rarer as their pores are less.' The intermingling of rarer with denser aether at the edges of opaque bodies allowed Newton to offer an explanation for the refraction of light into several colours as it passed them by. Newton went on to discuss other consequences of this aether, which he suggested might explain attraction and repulsion between bodies, and chemical reactions, especially between metals and acids. He also put forward a conjecture 'about [the] cause of gravity'. He argued that the descent of bodies under gravity might be caused by the pressure of the aether, which became denser as one moved further away from the centre of the earth.

H. W. Turnbull, J.F. Scott, A.R. Hall and Laura Tilling (eds), *The Correspondence of Isaac Newton*, 7 vols (Cambridge, 1959–77), vol. 2, 288–96 (which prints this letter).

Purchased from the Earl of Macclesfield by Cambridge University Library, August 2000.

46 CAMBRIDGE UNIVERSITY LIBRARY, MS. ADD. 4003, f. 22r
(figure 27)
19.4 × 15 cm
Bound notebook of 191 leaves

The first three folios of this notebook are blank. The next forty pages have been numbered by Newton, who also ruled the margins of folios four to thirty-one. The forty numbered pages (or twenty folios) were used at some point by Newton for the composition of an essay entitled 'De Gravitatione et aequipondio fluidorum et solidorum in fluidis' ('On the Gravity and Equal Weight of Fluid and Solid Bodies in Fluids'). The rest of the notebook was left blank.

'De gravitatione' is one of Newton's most important essays. It probably dates from winter 1684 or early spring 1685, since its contents suggest some familiarity with the tract 'De motu' but do not hint at the revisions that Newton soon made to it (see catalogue numbers 42 and 16). It provides the clearest evidence of Newton's break with Cartesian physics at the time of the composition of the *Principia*. Unusually careful and exact citations from Descartes' works accompany Newton's criticisms. Moreover, the argument of 'De gravitatione' depends in part on the results of pendulum experiments that Newton probably conducted during 1684. These experiments suggested that resistance due to penetration by the aether was very small, whereas, when he had written to Boyle in November 1679, Newton had believed that it was sufficient to explain the repulsion of one body by another (see catalogue number 45). In denying that motion might simply be the result of the pressure of small particles on larger bodies, Newton rejected Descartes' relative interpretation of matter and space. In its place, he suggested that space must be understood in absolute terms. Only infinite space and finite matter were compatible with divine creation. The pages from 'De gravitatione' that are on display (figure 27) illustrate this argument. In a discussion of non-elastic fluids, Newton proposed that 'compression does not cause a motion of the parts among themselves'. He went on to demonstrate this with the aid of a diagram that showed that 'moreover… all the parts exert pressure on each other equally and they do so with the same intensity of pressure as is exerted upon the external surface.'

The composition of 'De gravitatione' therefore represented a break with Newton's earlier writing about the aether. Although Newton decided that the straightforward effects of matter in motion could not explain the action of gravity, he did not abandon theories based on the aether entirely. Instead he modified them to take into account of his notion of force and continued to suspect that something like a rarefied aether might explain the behaviour of light, electricity, and other phenomena, perhaps including gravity itself.

A. Rupert Hall and Marie Boas Hall (eds), *Unpublished Scientific Papers of Isaac Newton* (Cambridge, 1962), pp. 89–156; John Herivel, *The Background to Newton's Principia* (Oxford, 1965), pp. 91–3, 219–235 [The Halls print and translate the entire text of 'De gravitatione'; Herivel prints and translates part of it. They all date the manuscript by appearance to the mid-1660s.]; Betty Jo Teeter Dobbs, *The Janus Faces of Genius* (Cambridge, 1991), pp. 139–46 [which convincingly redates the manuscript by content]; I. Bernard Cohen, *The Newtonian Revolution* (Cambridge, 1980), pp. 113–118; Robert Palter, 'Saving Newton's Text: Documents, Readers, and the Ways of the World', *Studies in History and Philosophy of Science*, 18 (1987), 385–439; Alan E. Shapiro, 'Light, Pressure, and Rectilinear Propagation: Descartes' Celestial Optics and Newton's Hydrostatics', *Studies in History and*

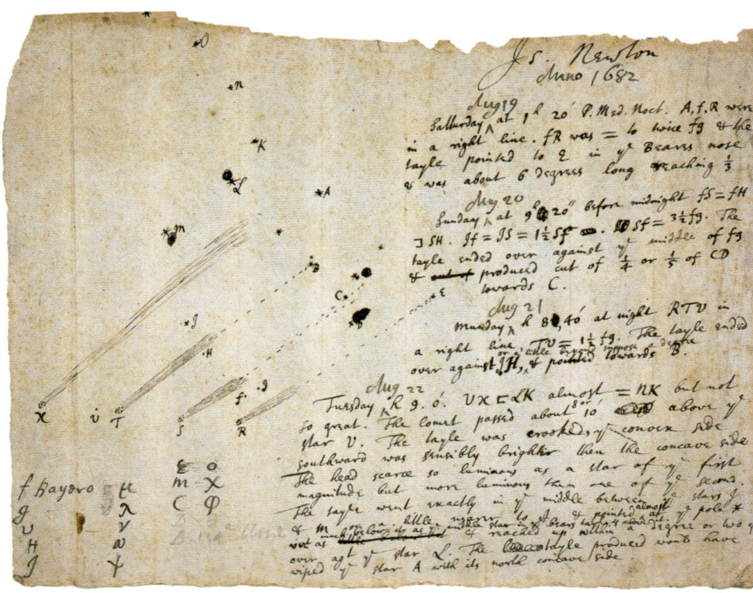

FIGURE 28
Newton's record of observations of the comet of 1682, written on a scrap of paper perhaps torn from a letter, University Library, Macclesfield Collection Box 43.

Philosophy of Science, 5 (1974), 239–96. [It is unlikely that the dating of this manuscript can be confirmed by the watermark (Arms of Amsterdam). Newton used paper with a similar watermark and no countermark in the late 1660s (see catalogue number 54). Paper with this watermark and the countermark 'AI' also appears in the mid-1670s (see catalogue number 28), and some sheets with another countermark can be found in catalogue numbers 52 (1680s or 1690s), and 16 (1685). Unfortunately, the binding of the notebook containing 'De gravitatione' is too tight to enable proper examination of the watermark, in particular for exact measurement or to identify any countermark. For discussion of dating by watermarks, see Alan E. Shapiro, 'Beyond the Dating Game: Watermark Clusters and the Composition of Newton's *Opticks*', in P.M. Harman and Alan E. Shapiro (eds), *The Investigation of Difficult Things* (Cambridge, 1992), pp. 181–227.]

Assessed 'Not fit to be printed' on behalf of Newton's executors by Thomas Pellet (25 September 1727); presented to Cambridge University Library by the fifth Earl of Portsmouth. See *A Catalogue of the Portsmouth Collection of Books and Papers written by or belonging to Sir Isaac Newton* (Cambridge, 1888), p. 48.

47 CAMBRIDGE UNIVERSITY LIBRARY, MACCLESFIELD COLLECTION BOX 43

(figure 28)

17.6 × 22.4 cm

This scrap of paper was presumably torn from the foot of a letter, since Newton's signature appears in the top right-hand corner. Beneath this, Newton has recorded observations of the comet of 1682 (see catalogue number 44) that he made on four successive nights, starting on 19 August. A very similar, but more complete, record appears in Newton's 'Waste Book' (see catalogue number 33). It seems reasonable to suppose that Newton originally wrote out his observations in the 'Waste Book' and subsequently communicated them to one of his correspondents, several of whom provided him with information about comets in the early 1680s. Robert Boyle (see catalogue number 45) wrote to Newton about '[the] Apparition of a Comet' on 19 August 1682, the day that Newton's observations began. In this letter, Boyle also commented that [the] darke weather joynd to my want of health, have for the two last nights kept me from lookeing after it.' It is tempting to suggest that Newton's account of his observations formed part of a reply to Boyle. However, the letter's recipient was presumably responsible for its subsequent annotations, of which those giving the dates are certainly in neither Newton's nor Boyle's hand.

H. W. Turnbull, J.F. Scott, A.R. Hall and Laura Tilling (eds), *The Correspondence of Isaac Newton*, 7 vols (Cambridge, 1959–77), vol. 2, 379–81 (which prints this manuscript); Richard S. Westfall, *Never at Rest. A Biography of Isaac Newton* (Cambridge, 1980), p. 396.

Purchased from the Earl of Macclesfield by Cambridge University Library, August 2000.

48 CAMBRIDGE UNIVERSITY LIBRARY, MS. ADD. 3965, f. 564v-5r
(figure 29)
29.5 × 19.1 cm

During the years between 1681 and 1686, Newton built up an extensive network of informants who provided him with observations of comets. The most prominent of these were John Flamsteed (see catalogue number 18), who sent Newton sightings from Greenwich, and Arthur Storer, who had been at school with Newton in Grantham and who had begun to send him astronomical information in 1678. Storer's observations were especially interesting since they were made in Maryland, New England. As the importance of calculations relating to the comet of 1680 grew with the composition of Book III of the *Principia*, Newton tried to obtain further corroboration of the observations available to him.

On 7 March 1681, Flamsteed had written a letter to be passed onto Newton in which he described a number of observations of the recent comet. He discussed the sightings made by Continental astronomers in both Paris and Rome, news of which had been sent to him by Halley (see catalogue number 42), and also mentioned 'an observation… made at Canterbury by one Hill an artificer with an instrument of 4 foot Radius on Friday morneing [November] 11'. At this stage, what interested Newton was to defend his belief that he had seen two comets in the winter skies of 1680 and 1681. By 19 September 1685, however, Newton was passionately anxious for information about the single comet of 1680–1, for which Flamsteed had earlier argued. He was trying to unravel the discrepancies between various accounts of the comet, which were complicated by the fact that different calendars were employed in England and on the Continent. He therefore applied to Flamsteed again for further information about the lowly Hill, whom he had ignored completely four and a half years earlier. Flamsteed drafted a reply on 25 September, attempting to help Newton sort matters out. He suggested

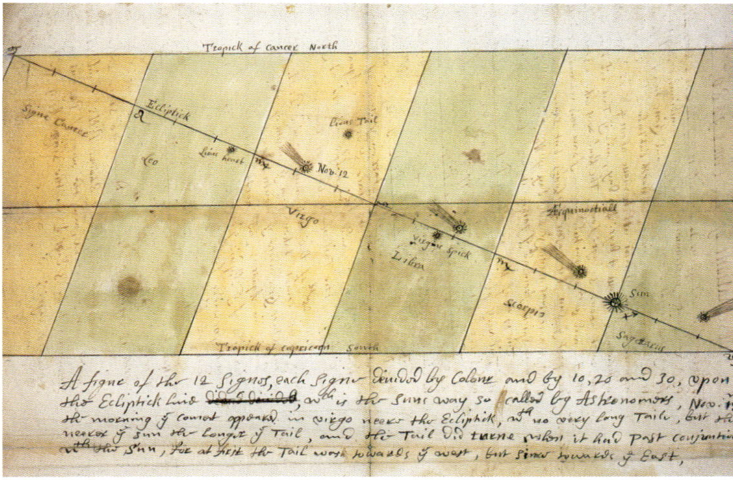

FIGURE 29
Observations on the comet of 1680 by Thomas Hill of Canterbury, perhaps sent to Newton by John Flamsteed in 1685, University Library, Ms. Add. 3965, f. 564v.

that 'As for the Canterbury observation it is a very course one. I discourst with the person that made it but found him a very ignorant well willer, yet I beleive his observations as good as those… made at Rome…' A version of this response was sent to Newton on 26 September, together with a letter that Hill had written to Flamsteed on 29 December 1681. This indicated that Hill had in fact first seen the comet on the morning of 12 November 1680 and revealed that he had continued to observe it until 3 January 1681, making a final sighting on 3 February.

The subject of this exchange between Flamsteed and Newton was Thomas Hill, a Canterbury artificer about whom no more is known. Hill's sightings of the comet of 1680–1 were communicated to Flamsteed at the Royal Observatory. Flamsteed later sent Newton more than a single letter from Hill. A drawing by Hill of the path of the comet through the heavens, accompanied by a detailed account of his 'Observations of the Comet 1680' (figure 29) can be found among the reports that Newton collected from that year.

H. W. Turnbull, J.F. Scott, A.R. Hall and Laura Tilling (eds), *The Correspondence of Isaac Newton*, 7 vols (Cambridge, 1959–77), vol. 2, 348–56, 372–3, 419–28; Eric G. Forbes, Lesley Murdin, and Frances Willmoth (eds), *The Correspondence of John Flamsteed*, 3 vols (Bristol, 1995–2001), vol. 1, 749, 772, 843–4, 925; vol. 2, 245–56.

Presented to Cambridge University Library by the fifth Earl of Portsmouth. See *A Catalogue of the Portsmouth Collection of Books and Papers written by or belonging to Sir Isaac Newton* (Cambridge, 1888), p. 4–5.

49 CAMBRIDGE UNIVERSITY LIBRARY, MS. ADD. 3982, NUMBER 6
30.2 × 18.8 cm

Newton's calculations in Book III of the first edition of the *Principia* had demonstrated that comets travelled in parabolic paths. During the mid-1690s, Edmond Halley (see catalogue number 42) began to recalculate some of Newton's data and to demonstrate that some cometary orbits at least were elliptical. One consequence of this was the realisation that particular comets might have appeared previously in the historical record. The easiest of these comets to identify turned out to be that of 1682, subsequently known as 'Halley's Comet', which Halley was quickly able to compare with the comet of 1607. Although it took Halley many more years to develop in full his prediction of the return of this comet, the popularity of this idea among Newton's disciples suggested that it chimed well with their master's attempts to give a single account of nature, history, and theology.

Halley's calculations in the mid-1690s depended on information provided by others, just as Newton's had done in the mid-1680s. Flamsteed in particular shared his observations with the two men who were subsequently to become the bane of his life.

In August 1695, Halley began by working out the orbit of the comet of 1683. He soon considered that of 1664 (see catalogue number 2), where he was hampered by the lack of sufficiently accurate observations, and suggested that he might also tackle the observations of 1680–1. By the end of September, Halley had made corrections to the information that Newton had used in the *Principia* and had improved on Newton's description of the line of the comet through arithmetical calculation. He wrote that 'I find certain indication of an Elliptick Orb in that Comet and am satisfied that it will be very difficult to hit it exactly by a Parabolick.' In a letter of 17 October, Newton indicated that Halley's reasoning had now convinced him, although he supplied numerous corrections to the calculations. Halley welcomed these in his letter of 21 October (on display), in which he also mentioned his ideas about the comet of 1682.

The calculations that Halley provided for Newton eventually made their way into the second edition of the *Principia* (see catalogue number 44). Halley's work also encouraged Newton to reconsider the effects of the gravitation of the planets on cometary orbits. It was thus related to the ideas that Newton put forward in his treatment of the motion of the moon (see catalogue number 19). Newton's reliance on Halley is revealing in other ways. Firstly, it illustrates the extent to which Newton by the 1690s depended on younger men to enforce the mathematical rigour for which he had once been famous. It also highlights the collaborative nature of the final Newtonian synthesis, despite the very solitary methods of Newton's own original work. Furthermore, Newton's acceptance of Halley's assistance draws attention to some of the problems that confronted him in the 1690s. In that decade of theological paranoia, when accusations of atheism or deism were rife, Halley's friendship was to some extent a liability because of the reputation for immoral behaviour that he had acquired. This may account for Newton's reluctance to support Halley in the contest for the Savilian chair of astronomy at Oxford in 1691, when David Gregory was elected. Yet the readiness to court controversy displayed by Newton's younger friends in general helps to explain why he retreated from publishing many of the bolder statements that he had advanced in private during the 1690s, despite the success of the *Principia*.

H. W. Turnbull, J.F. Scott, A.R. Hall and Laura Tilling (eds), *The Correspondence of Isaac Newton*, 7 vols (Cambridge, 1959–77), vol. 4, 165–83 (part of which prints this letter); Alan Cook, *Edmond Halley* (Oxford, 1998), pp. 205–17; I. Bernard Cohen, *The Newtonian Revolution* (Cambridge, 1980), pp. 269–71.

Presented to Cambridge University Library by the fifth Earl of Portsmouth. See *A Catalogue of the Portsmouth Collection of Books and Papers written by or belonging to Sir Isaac Newton* (Cambridge, 1888), p. 36.

50 CAMBRIDGE UNIVERSITY LIBRARY, MS. ADD. 3974, f. 2bv
(figure 30)
20.4 × 16 cm

There were other forces at work in the world besides gravity. One of these was magnetism, which together with electricity exhibited the patterns of attraction and repulsion that occupied Newton for much of his life. Electricity only began to excite Newton's serious interest as a result of experiments performed at the Royal Society during his presidency of that body. Ideas derived from electrical investigations were included in the queries to the *Opticks*, especially in those added to the second edition (see catalogue numbers 29 and 30). Newton himself never made any serious observations of electrical phenomena. This was also true of magnetism, although mentions of magnets and lodestones

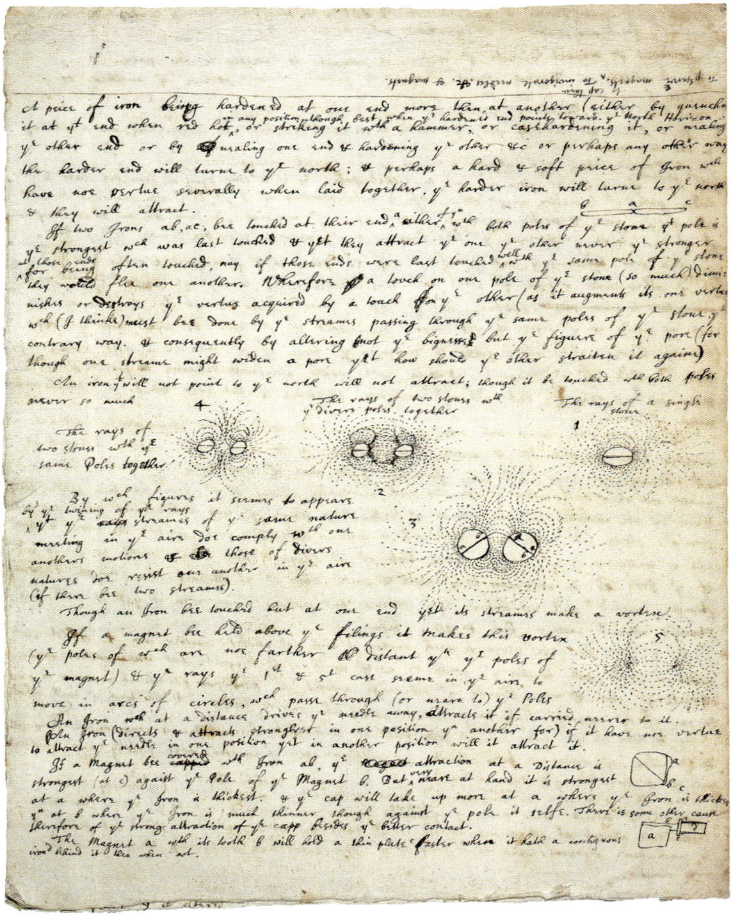

FIGURE 30
Newton's experiments with magnets and iron filings, University Library, Ms. Add. 3974, f. 2bv.

occur sporadically in Newton's writings. A magnet was among his purchases in 1667 (see catalogue number 3), but he owned few books related to magnetism. In the mid-1660s, Newton had entered several queries about 'Atraction Magneticall' into his philosophical notebook (see catalogue number 2). His main concern seems to have been to consider whether a stream of magnetic particles might be employed to turn a perpetual motion machine. Some years later, however, perhaps towards the end of the 1660s or even in the early 1670s, Newton attempted a slightly more complete investigation of magnetic attraction. After making notes on the history of compasses and the manufacture of magnets, he explored the simple properties of attraction and repulsion in hammered iron magnets. He also conducted rather more extensive experiments with lodestones, attempting to map the pattern of their interactions using iron filings (figure 30).

These were basic observations that repeated work that was already standard in the philosophical literature about magnetism. Despite this, Newton's work on magnets had obvious relevance for his investigation of the causes of other natural phenomena. Experiments with magnets and iron filings seem at first to have confirmed the idea that a stream of active particles moving in a particular direction might be responsible for the effects that Newton described: '[the] ~~rays~~ streames of [the] same nature meeting in [the] aire doe comply [with] one anothers motions & those of divers natures doe resist one another in [the] aire.' This was very similar to the language with which Newton sought to explain the behaviour of light in the early 1670s and which he used when investigating the swing of pendulums at that time. Newton continued to deploy magnetic analogies in his later work on the aether and in his attempts to explain the gravity. But as he moved away from Cartesian or material explanations the relevance of these simple magnetic experiments decreased.

J.E. McGuire and Martin Tamny (eds), *Certain Philosophical Questions: Newton's Trinity Notebook* (Cambridge, 1983), pp. 377–9.

Presented to Cambridge University Library by the fifth Earl of Portsmouth. See *A Catalogue of the Portsmouth Collection of Books and Papers written by or belonging to Sir Isaac Newton* (Cambridge, 1888), pp. 19–20.

51 CAMBRIDGE UNIVERSITY LIBRARY, MS. ADD. 3970, f. 619r
30.1 × 18.5 cm

This draft for the final query (23) of the *Opticks* was probably composed in autumn or winter 1705. It differed substantially from the published query as it appeared in the Latin *Optice* of the following year. In particular, it began with a direct allusion to the atomist philosophy of the ancients, that by the mid-1680s Newton supposed to be a precursor of his own. It also suggested that an omnipresent God was himself the cause of gravity, since 'matter depends upon a Deity for its laws of motion as well as for its existence'. The draft attempted to explain how Newton's revival of ancient theories of divine harmony differed from Cartesian attempts to make 'God the author of all motion'. Newton's distinctions did not impress contemporary Continental philosophers. In particular, the suggestion that 'all space be the sensorium of a thinking being', when it appeared along with some of the other material from this draft in the published Query 20, excited Leibniz to argue that Newton had made God dependent on space as an organ through which he might perceive creation.

Few people understood the explanations that Newton now gave for the activity of light and gravity. David Gregory, who saw the new queries for the *Opticks* in draft in December 1705, commented that Newton had 'shewed that Light is neither a communication of motion nor of a Pressure. He inclines to believe it to be projected minute bodys.' The folio on display gives some indication of the difficulty that Newton found in demonstrating the affinity between his natural philosophy and ancient ideas of 'actuating matter harmonicaly by the God Pan's playing upon a Pipe& attributing musick to the spheres'. It bears extensive signs of correction and rewriting and was never published in anything like this form. Nevertheless, it provides a clear indication of Newton's persistence with explanations for the function of gravity that he had begun to develop in the mid-1680s (see catalogue number 43 and 44).

J.E. McGuire and P.M. Rattansi, 'Newton and the "Pipes of Pan"', *Notes and Records of the Royal Society of London*, 21 (1966), 108–143; J.E. McGuire, *Tradition and Innovation. Newton's Metaphysics of Nature* (Dordrecht, 1995), pp. 190–238; W.G. Hiscock (ed.), *David Gregory, Isaac Newton and their Circle* (Oxford, 1937), pp. 29–30.

Presented to Cambridge University Library by the fifth Earl of Portsmouth. See *A Catalogue of the Portsmouth Collection of Books and Papers written by or belonging to Sir Isaac Newton* (Cambridge, 1888), pp. 9–10.

FIGURE 31
Newton's rooms in Trinity College, on the first floor to the right of the gatehouse, from David Loggan's *Cantabrigia illustrata* (1690), University Library, Ii 9.3.

FROM LIBRARY TO LABORATORY

Newton started to read and make extracts from alchemical texts in the late 1660s. He soon began to carry out experiments for himself, in a laboratory that he had constructed at Trinity, and he amassed a substantial alchemical library. Quite apart from the intrinsic appeal of the quest for the transmutation of metals, alchemy offered answers to several questions that bothered Newton elsewhere in his work. The transformations in form, appearance, and perhaps even essence achieved by alchemical experiment seemed to reveal much about the composition and structure of matter. They also suggested how active forces might operate within and between material bodies. Alchemical ideas may even have informed the concept of divine action that Newton developed. They certainly provided him with evidence to support his belief that philosophical and religious truth was the preserve of a virtuous minority. The investigation of the mysteries of chemical transformation was perhaps Newton's principal activity in the years from the early 1670s until the mid-1690s.

52 KING'S COLLEGE, CAMBRIDGE, KEYNES MS. 32, P. 3
(figure 32)
21 × 16.3 cm

Michael Maier (1569–1622) was one of the alchemical writers who most influenced Newton and his contemporaries. Newton had copies of nine separate publications by Maier in his library (see catalogue number 53) and made a substantial manuscript anthology from Maier's work (figure 32), as well as copying other shorter passages. He was familiar with the text of Maier's *Symbola aureae mensae duodecim nationum* (Frankfurt, 1617) as early as the late 1660s, but probably copied the extracts from it that are on display in the 1680s or early 1690s. These provide a summary of book two of Maier's work, in particular his account of the alchemy of

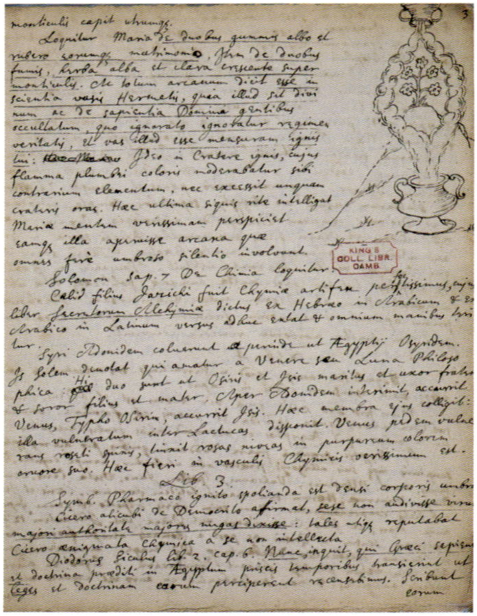

FIGURE 32
Extracts from the work of the alchemist, Michael Maier, King's College, Cambridge, Keynes Ms. 32, p. 3.

Maria the Jewess, supposedly the sister of Moses and teacher of the princes of the Egyptians. According to Maier, who made her one of the twelve wisest philosophers, Maria spoke of the marriage of male and female elements through fire and in the smoke given off from 'the Hermetic vase'. This may perhaps have been a reference to the sublimation of black lead sulphide (PbS) to create yellow lead oxide (PbO), a process with which Newton could have been familiar from his many experiments with lead compounds and amalgams from the 1670s onwards (although see also catalogue number 53).

The history of alchemy that Maier provided in the *Symbola* was particularly important for the development of Newton's alchemical reading and research. Maier's work was one of the principal sources used by Newton to compile a list of chemical authors, perhaps in the early 1670s, which he continued to amend and expand into the 1690s. Although by no means a catalogue of Newton's alchemical library, this list and its successors certainly represented an assessment of those books that it would be desirable for a practising alchemist to read and own. Maier's influence was especially apparent in the increasing emphasis given in Newton's library to ancient and medieval alchemical authors during the 1680s and 1690s.

Karin Figala, John Harrison, and Ulrich Petzold, '*De Scriptoribus Chemicis*: Sources for the Establishment of Isaac Newton's (Al)chemical Library', in P.M. Harman and Alan E. Shapiro (eds), *The Investigation of Difficult Things* (Cambridge, 1992), pp. 135–79; John Harrison, *The Library of Isaac Newton* (Cambridge, 1978), pp. 188–9; Ulrich Neumann, 'Maier, Michael', and Heike Hild, 'Maria', both in Claus Priesner and Karin Figala (eds), *Alchemie: Lexikon einer hermetischen Wissenschaft* (Munich, 1998), pp. 232–6; Betty Jo Teeter Dobbs, *The Janus Faces of Genius* (Cambridge, 1991), pp. 122–3.

Sotheby sale, 13 July 1936, lot 43; purchased by Gabriel Wells for £34. J.M. Keynes wrote to Wells to ask about this manuscript on 25 August 1936 and was offered it for a ten percent commission by Wells on 4 September. The transaction was completed on 8 September.

53 MICHAEL MAIER, *Secretioris naturae secretorum scrutinium chymicum* (Frankfurt, 1687)

(figure 33)

4°: π⁴, A–T⁴

16.6 × 11.2 cm

Trinity College, Cambridge, shelfmark NQ 16/88

This book is one of nine separately published works by Maier that were in Newton's library at his death. Newton has marked numerous passages (see figure 33) by turning down the corners of the relevant pages. The

FIGURE 33
Newton's copy of Michael Maier, *Secretioris naturae secretorum scrutinium chymicum* (Frankfurt, 1687), Trinity College, Cambridge, NQ 16/88, pp. 64-5.

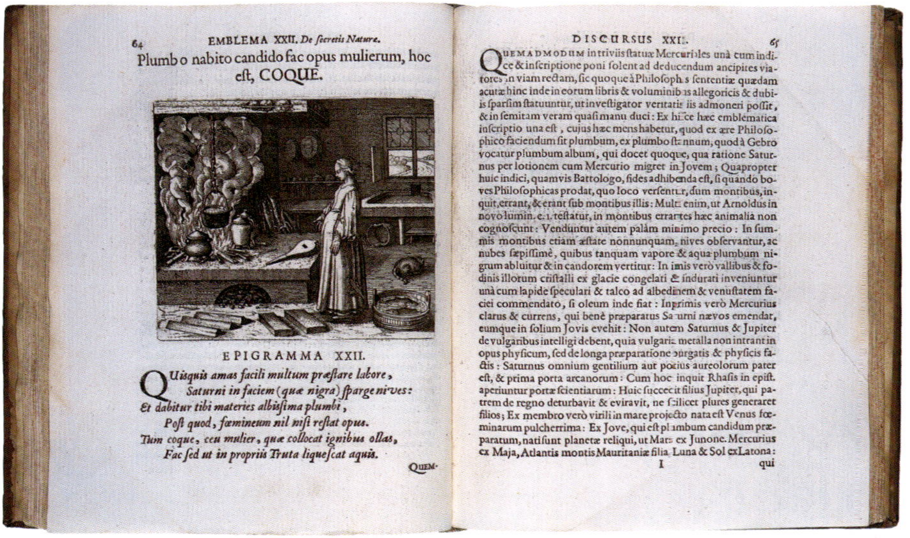

64 EMBLEMA XXII. *De secretis Naturæ.*

Plumbo nabito candido fac opus mulierum, hoc eſt, COQUE.

EPIGRAMMA XXII.

Quisquis amas facili multum præſtare labore,
Saturni in faciem (quæ nigra) ſparge nives:
Et dabitur tibi materies albiſſima plumbi,
Poſt quod, fœmineum nil niſi reſtat opus.
Tum coque, ceu mulier, quæ collocat ignibus ollas,
Fac ſed ut in propriis Truta liqueſcat aquis.

QUEM-

DISCURSUS XXII. 65

QUEMADMODUM in triviis ſtatuæ Mercuriales unà cum indice & inſcriptione poni ſolent ad deducendum ancipites viatores in viam rectam, ſic quoque à Philoſophis ſententiæ quædam acutæ hinc inde in eorum libris & voluminibus allegoricis & dubiis ſparſim ſtatuuntur, ut inveſtigator veritatis iis admoneri poſſit, & in ſemitam veram quaſi manu duci: Ex hisce hæc emblematica inſcriptio una eſt, cujus hæc mens habetur, quod ex ære Philoſophico faciendum ſit plumbum, ex plumbo ſtannum, quod à Gebro vocatur plumbum album, qui docet quoque, qua ratione Saturnus per lotionem cum Mercurio migret in Jovem; Quapropter huic indici, quamvis Battologo, fides adhibenda eſt, ſi quando boves Philoſophicas prodat, quo loco verſentur, dum montibus, inquit, errant, & erant ſub montibus illis: Multæ enim, ut Arnoldus in novo lumin. c. 1. teſtatur, in montibus errantes hæc animalia non cognoſcunt: Venduntur autem palàm minimo precio: In ſummis montibus etiam æſtate nonnunquam, nives obſervantur, ac nubes ſæpiſſimè, quibus tanquam vapore & aqua plumbum nigrum abluitur & in candorem vertitur: In imis verò vallibus & fodinis illorum criſtalli ex glacie congelati & indurati inveniuntur unà cum lapide ſpeculari & talco ad albedinem & venuſtatem faciei commendato, ſi oleum inde fiat: Inprimis verò Mercurius clarus & currens, qui benè præparatus Saturni nævos emendat, eumque in ſolium Jovis evehit: Non autem Saturnus & Jupiter de vulgaribus intelligi debent, quia vulgaria metalla non intrant in opus phyſicum, ſed de longa præparatione purgatis & phyſicis factis: Saturnus omnium gentilium aut potius aureolorum pater eſt, & prima porta arcanorum: Cum hoc inquit Rhaſis in epiſt. aperiuntur portæ ſcientiarum: Huic ſuccedit filius Jupiter, qui patrem de regno deturbavit & eviravit, ne ſcilicet plures generaret filios; Ex membro verò virili in mare projecto nata eſt Venus fœminarum pulcherrima: Ex Jove, qui eſt plumbum candidum præparatum, nati ſunt planetæ reliqui, ut Mars ex Junone. Mercurius ex Maja, Atlantis montis Mauritaniæ filia. Luna & Sol ex Latona:

I qui

opening on display (pp. 64–5), which is also indicated in this manner, discusses the transformation of so-called black lead into a pure white substance and its subsequent refinement through 'cooking' or heating. According to Maier, these were stages in the manufacture and purification of the philosopher's stone. Maier cites works supposedly by the Arabic alchemists, Geber and Rhazes, and appears to refer to a series of amalgamations of lead, tin, and other metallic compounds. In his experiments of the 1680s (see catalogue number 14), Newton was often concerned with the combination of lead and salts of tin leading to changes in the form of both substances.

John Harrison, *The Library of Isaac Newton* (Cambridge, 1978), p. 188.

Listed by the booksellers who appraised Newton's library for his executors; bought with the rest of the library by John Huggins in 1727. Bookplate of Charles Huggins. Bookplate of James Musgrave, with shelfmark C1–8. Presented to Trinity College, Cambridge, on 30 October 1943 by the Pilgrim Trust.

54 KING'S COLLEGE, CAMBRIDGE, KEYNES MS. 62, f. 4r
(figure 34)
19.7 × 15.6 cm

Newton began reading alchemical books in the late 1660s. In 1669, he recorded that he had spent £1. 8s. on the *Theatrum chemicum* (1659–61), a six volume compendium of chemical works edited by Lazarus Zetzner (see catalogue number 3). At about this time, he also acquired a small volume containing copies of a number of miscellaneous alchemical texts in manuscript. Many of these texts had appeared in print. Some could be found in the *Theatrum chemicum*; several were included in Elias Ashmole's *Theatrum chemicum Britannicum* (1652); others had been published separately or in other collections. Newton often kept extracts from printed books in small notebooks made by folding a sheet of paper into four. He treated his collection of alchemical manuscripts in a similar way, making extracts of particular works in the sheet of notes on display. In addition to copying the text of 'The breif of Sr Edward Vere his book', Newton also made drawings of the vessels and furnace recommended by the author for the distillation of mercury.

Betty Jo Teeter Dobbs, *The Foundations of Newton's Alchemy* (Cambridge, 1975), pp. 88, 132, 137; King's College, Cambridge, Keynes Ms. 67.

Sotheby sale, 13 July 1936, lot 108; purchased by Maggs Brothers for £16. Offered to J.M. Keynes for a twenty percent commission on 30 July 1936.

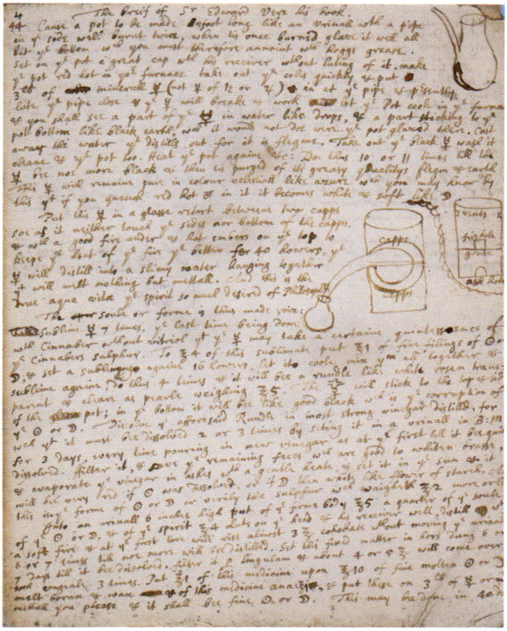

FIGURE 34
Drawings of chemical apparatus from Newton's notes, King's College, Cambridge, Keynes Ms. 62, f. 4r.

55 RETORT AND CRUCIBLE
Museum of the History of Science, Oxford

Newton would have used pieces of apparatus similar to these in his chemical experiments (see catalogue number 54). Tall, triangular crucibles are known to have been existed from the sixteenth century and were being manufactured by John Dwight at Fulham in the 1670s and 1680s. They were often used for the heating of metals in the laboratory. Stoneware retorts were widely employed for distillation.

The examples of these objects that are on display were excavated from the rear of the Museum of the History of Science in Oxford, originally the site of the museum founded by Elias Ashmole and opened to the public in 1683. The basement of this building was used as a laboratory in the late seventeenth century. The design of these vessels was long lived, however, and they could equally well date from the mid-eighteenth century.

J.A. Bennett, S.A. Johnston, A.V. Simcock, *Solomon's House in Oxford. New Finds from the First Museum* (Oxford, 2000), pp. 30–47.

10 I was in the Spirit on the Lords day, and heard behind me a great voice, as of a trumpet,

11 Saying, I am Alpha and Omega, the firſt and the laſt: and, what thou ſeeſt, write in a book, and ſend *it* unto the ſeven churches which are in Aſia; unto Epheſus, and unto Smyrna, and unto Pergamos, and unto Thyatira, and unto Sardis, and unto Philadelphia, and unto Laodicea.

12 And I turned to ſee the voice that ſpake with me. And being turned, I ſaw ſeven golden candleſticks.

13 And in the midſt of the ſeven candleſticks, *one* like unto the Son of man, * clothed ‖ with a garment down to the foot, and girt about the paps with a golden girdle.

14 His head and *his* hairs *were* white like wool, as white as ſnow; and his eyes *were* as a flame of fire.

15 And his feet like unto fine braſs, † as if they burned in a furnace; and his voice as the ſound of many waters.

16 And he had in his right hand ſeven ſtars: and out of his mouth went a ſharp two-edged ſword: and his countenance *was* as the ſun ſhineth in his ſtrength.

17 And when I ſaw him, I fell at his feet as dead: and he laid his right hand upon me, ſaying unto me, Fear not, * I am the firſt and the laſt:

18 I *am* he that liveth, and was dead; and behold, I am alive for evermore, Amen; and have the keys of hell and of death.

19 Write the things which thou haſt ſeen, and the things which are, and the things which ſhall be hereafter.

20 The myſtery of the ſeven ſtars which thou ſaweſt in my right hand, and the ſeven golden candleſticks. The ſeven ſtars * are the angels of the ſeven churches; and the ſeven candleſticks which thou ſaweſt, are the ſeven churches.

* Dan. 10.5,6. ‖ Or, with a robe. Exod. 28.4,31. † Gr. as having been refined in a furnace. * Iſa. 41.4. & 44.6. * Matth. 20.20.

CHAP. II.

What is commanded to be written to the angels, (that is, the miniſters) of the churches of 1 Epheſus, 8 Smyrna, 12 Pergamos, 18 Thyatira: and what is commended, or found wanting in them.

UNto the angel of the church of Epheſus, write, Theſe things ſaith he that holdeth the ſeven ſtars in his right hand, who walketh in the midſt of the ſeven golden candleſticks:

2 I know thy works, and thy labor, and thy patience, and how thou canſt not bear them which are evil: and thou haſt tried them which ſay they are apoſtles, and are not; and haſt found them liars:

3 And haſt born, and haſt patience, and for my names ſake haſt labored, and haſt not fainted.

4 Nevertheleſs, I have *ſomewhat* againſt thee, becauſe thou haſt left thy firſt love.

5 Remember therefore from whence thou art fallen, and repent, and do the firſt works; or elſe I will come unto thee quickly, and will remove thy candleſtick out of his place, except thou repent.

6 But this thou haſt, that thou hateſt the deeds of the Nicolaitanes, which I alſo hate.

7 He that hath an ear, let him hear what the Spirit ſaith unto the churches, To him that overcometh will I give to eat of the tree of life, which is in the midſt of the ‖ paradiſe of God.

8 ¶ And unto the angel of the church in Smyrna, write, Theſe things ſaith the firſt and the laſt, which was dead, and is alive;

9 I know thy works, and tribulation, and poverty, (but thou art rich) and *I know* the blaſphemy of them who ſay they are Jews, and are not, but *are* the ſynagogue of Satan.

10 Fear none of thoſe things which thou ſhalt ſuffer: behold, the devil ſhall caſt *ſome* of you into priſon, that ye may be tried; and ye ſhall have tribulation ten days: be thou faithful unto death, and I will give thee a crown of life.

11 He that hath an ear, let him hear what the Spirit ſaith unto the churches, He that overcometh, ſhall not be hurt of the ſecond death.

12 ¶ And to the angel of the church in Pergamos, write, Theſe things ſaith he, who hath the ſharp ſword with two edges,

13 I know thy works, and where thou dwelleſt, *even* where Satans † ſeat *is*: and thou holdeſt faſt my name, and haſt not denied my faith, even in thoſe days wherein Antipas *was* my faithful martyr, who was ſlain among you, where Satan dwelleth.

14 But I have a few things againſt thee, becauſe thou haſt there them that hold the doctrine of * Balaam, who taught Balac to caſt a ſtumbling-block before the children of Iſrael, to eat things ſacrificed unto idols, and to commit fornication.

15 So haſt thou alſo them that hold the doctrine of the Nicolaitanes, which thing I hate.

16 Repent; or elſe I will come unto thee quickly, and will fight againſt them with the ſword of my mouth.

17 He that hath an ear, let him hear what the Spirit ſaith unto the churches. To him that overcometh will I give to eat of the hidden manna, and will give him a white ſtone, and in the ſtone a new name written, which no man knoweth, ſaving he that receiveth *it*.

18 ¶ And unto the angel of the church in Thyatira, write, Theſe things ſaith the Son of God, who hath his eyes like unto a flame of fire, and his feet *are* like fine braſs;

19 I know thy works, and charity, and ſervice, and faith, and thy patience, and thy works; and the laſt *to be* more then the firſt.

20 Notwithſtanding, I have a few things againſt thee, becauſe thou ſuffereſt that woman * Jezabel, which calleth her ſelf a propheteſs, to teach and to ſeduce my ſervants to commit fornication, and to eat things ſacrificed unto idols.

21 And I gave her ſpace to repent of her fornication, and ſhe repented not.

22 Behold, I will caſt her into a bed, and them that commit adultery with her into great tribulation, except they repent of their deeds.

23 And I will kill her children with death: and all the churches ſhall know that * I am he which ſearcheth the reins and hearts; and I will give unto every one of you according to your works.

24 But unto you I ſay, and unto the reſt in Thyatira, as many as have not this doctrine, & which have not known the depths of Satan (as they ſpeak) I will put upon you none other burden,

25 But that which ye have *already*, hold faſt till I come.

26 And he that overcometh, and keepeth my works unto the end, to him will I give power over the nations.

27 (* And he ſhall rule them with a rod of iron: as the veſſels of a potter † ſhall they be broken to ſhivers) even as I received of my Father.

28 And I will give him the morning ſtar.

29 He that hath an ear, let him hear what the Spirit ſaith unto the churches.

† Gr. throne. * Numb. 25.1. & 31.16. * 1 King. 16.31. * Pſal. 7.9. Jer. 11.20. & 17.10. * Pſal. 2.9. † Gr. are broken.

CHAP. III.

2 The angel of the church of Sardis is reproved, 3 exhorted to repent, and threatned if he do not repent. 8 The angel of the church of Philadelphia, 10 is approved for his diligence and patience. 15 The angel of Laodicea is rebuked, for being neither hot nor cold, 19 and admoniſhed to be more zealous. 20 Chriſt ſtandeth at the door, and knocketh.

AND unto the angel of the church in Sardis, write, Theſe things ſaith he that hath the ſeven Spirits of God, and the ſeven ſtars; I know thy works, that thou haſt a name that thou liveſt, and art dead.

2 Be watchful, and ſtrengthen the things which remain, that are ready to die: for I have not found thy works perfect before God.

3 Remember therefore how thou haſt received and heard, and hold faſt, and repent. * If therefore thou ſhalt not watch, I will come on thee as a thief, and thou ſhalt not know what hour I will come upon thee.

4 Thou haſt a few names even in Sardis, which have not defiled their garments; and they ſhall walk with me in white: for they are worthy.

5 He that overcometh, the ſame ſhall be clothed in white raiment; and I will not blot out his name out of the * book of life, but I will confeſs his name before my Father, and before his angels.

6 He that hath an ear, let him hear what the Spirit ſaith unto the churches.

7 ¶ And to the angel of the church in Philadelphia, write, Theſe things ſaith he *that is* holy, he *that is* true, he that hath * the key of David, he that openeth, and no man ſhutteth; and ſhutteth, and no man openeth:

8 I know thy works: behold, I have ſet before thee an open door, and no *man* can ſhut it: for thou haſt a little ſtrength, and haſt kept my word, and haſt not denied my name.

9 Behold, I will make them of the ſynagogue of Satan (which ſay they are Jews, and are not, but do lie) behold, I will make them to come and worſhip before thy feet, and to know that I have loved thee.

10 Becauſe thou haſt kept the word of my patience, I alſo will keep thee from the hour of temptation, which ſhall come upon all the world to try them that dwell upon the earth.

11 Behold, I come quickly: hold that faſt which thou haſt, that no man take thy crown.

12 Him that overcometh, will I make a pillar in the temple of my God, and he ſhall go no more out: and I will write upon him the name of my God, and the name of the city of my God, *which is* new Jeruſalem, which cometh down out of heaven from my God: and *I will write upon him* my new name.

13 He that hath an ear, let him hear what the Spirit ſaith unto the churches.

14 ¶ And unto the angel of the church ‖ of the Laodiceans, write, Theſe things ſaith the Amen, the faithful and true witneſs, the beginning of the creation of God;

15 I know thy works, that thou art neither cold nor hot: I would thou wert cold or hot.

16 So then becauſe thou art luke-warm, and neither cold nor hot, I will ſpue thee out of my mouth:

17 Becauſe thou ſayeſt, I am rich, and increaſed with goods, and have need of nothing; and knoweſt not that thou art wretched, and miſerable, and poor, and blind, and naked.

18 I counſel thee to buy of me gold tried in the fire, that thou mayeſt be rich; and white raiment, that thou mayeſt be clothed, and *that* the ſhame of thy nakedneſs do not appear; and anoint thine eyes with eye-ſalve, that thou mayeſt ſee.

19 * As many as I love, I rebuke and chaſten, be zealous therefore and repent.

20 Behold, I ſtand at the door, and knock; if any man hear my voice, and open the door, I will come in to him, and will ſup with him, and he with me.

21 To him that overcometh will I grant to ſit with me in my throne, even as I alſo overcame, and am ſet down with my Father in his throne.

22 He that hath an ear, let him hear what the Spirit ſaith unto the churches.

* Prov. 3.11. Heb. 12.5.

CHAP. IV.

2 John ſeeth the throne of God in heaven. 4 The four and twenty elders. 6 The four beaſts full of eyes before and behind. 10 The elders lay down their crowns, and worſhip him that ſat on the throne.

AFter this I looked, and behold, a door was opened in heaven: and the firſt voice which I heard, was as it were of a trumpet talking with me; which ſaid, Come up hither, and I will ſhew thee things which muſt be hereafter.

2 And immediately I was in the ſpirit: and behold, a throne was ſet in heaven, and *one* ſat on the throne.

3 And he that ſat, was to look upon like a jaſper, and a ſardine ſtone: and *there was* a rainbow round about the throne, in ſight like unto an emerald.

4 And round about the throne *were* four and twenty † ſeats: and upon the ſeats I ſaw four and twenty elders ſitting, clothed in white raiment; and they had on their heads crowns of gold.

5 And out of the throne proceeded lightnings, and thundrings, and voices. And *there were* ſeven lamps of fire burning before the throne, which are the ſeven Spirits of God.

6 And before the throne *there was* * a ſea of glaſs like unto cryſtal, and in the midſt of the throne, and round about the throne, *were* four † beaſts full of eyes, before and behind.

7 And the firſt beaſt *was* like a lion, and the ſecond beaſt like a calf, and the third beaſt had a face like a man, and the fourth beaſt *was* like a flying eagle.

8 † And the four beaſts had each of them ſix wings about him, and *they were* full of eyes within; and † they reſt not day and night, ſaying, * Holy, holy, holy, Lord God almighty, which was, and is, and is to come.

9 And when † thoſe beaſts give glory, and honour and thanks to him that † ſat on the throne, who liveth for ever and ever,

10 The four and twenty elders fall down before him that ſat on the throne, and worſhip him that liveth for ever and ever, and caſt their crowns before the throne, ſaying,

11 * Thou art worthy, O Lord, to receive glory, and honour, and power: for thou haſt created all things, and for thy pleaſure they are, and were created.

† gr. thrones. * 1 Kings 7.23. † gr. living creatures. † gr. and four living creatures. † gr. they have no reſt. * Iſa. 6.3. † gr. the living creatures. † gr. ſitteth.

CHAP. V.

1 The book ſealed with ſeven ſeals: 5, 6, 7, which onely the Lamb that was ſlain is worthy to open. 8 Therefore the elders praiſe him, 9 and confeſs that he redeemed them with his blood. 11, 12 The Angels alſo praiſe the Lamb.

AND I ſaw in the right hand of him that ſat on the throne, a book written within, and on the backſide, ſealed with ſeven ſeals.

2 And I ſaw a ſtrong angel proclaiming with a loud voice, Who is worthy to open the book, and to looſe the ſeales thereof?

3 And † no man in heaven, nor in earth, neither under the earth, was able to open the book, neither to look thereon.

4 And

DUTY AND DOMINION

FIGURE 35
One of Newton's copies of the Bible, with his annotations on the Book of Revelation, Trinity College, Cambridge, Adv.d.1.10, sig. 2Z6v-7r.

Both as mathematician and as alchemist, Newton showed deep respect for antiquity. During the 1680s, his reading of theology also encouraged him to believe in historical links between the ideas of the ancient Hebrews, the geometry of classical Greece, and the divinity of the true Christian Church, which had been corrupted by monks and by the Papacy. These beliefs took shape in a series of 'scholia' or clarifications that Newton composed for the *Principia* during the 1690s. In the end, he decided to omit most of them from the second edition of the *Principia* (1713), but incorporated some of their ideas in its 'Scholium Generale'. There he tried to set out the metaphysical implications of his work in a way that reflected the nature of his beliefs. The fullest expression of Newton's sense of antiquity, however, remained in his theological writing. Using both secular and biblical history, and concentrating in particular on those events that appeared to be the fulfilment of prophecies, Newton reconstructed the history of the Church. He did so in a way that vindicated his own increasingly heretical creed, especially his rejection of the divinity of Christ and of the Holy Ghost. These convictions, which derived in part from the moral and biblical literalism of his puritan upbringing, now underpinned both his interpretation of the natural world and his account of human history.

56 CAMBRIDGE UNIVERSITY LIBRARY, MS. ADD. 3965, f. 268r
31.3 × 19.3 cm

When he visited Cambridge during the first week of May 1694, David Gregory recorded several pieces of news about Newton's intentions for a second edition of the *Principia*. He noted that 'He will spread himself in exhibiting the agreement of this philosophy with that of the Ancients and principally with that of Thales. The philosophy of Epicurus and Lucretius is true and old, but was wrongly interpreted by the ancients as atheism.' During the early 1690s, Newton indeed spent much time drafting clarifications or 'scholia' to his arguments at the start of Book III of the *Principia* (see catalogue numbers 43 and 44). One of the most difficult of these proved to be the 'scholium' that he decided to write for proposition VII, corollary 2: 'Gravity towards the individual equal particles of a body is inversely as the square of the distance from those particles'.

Newton wished to argue that the ancient atomist philosophers had shared his understanding of gravity. This knowledge had reached them from the mystical philosophy of the Egyptians and Phoenicians, who had learned it from Moses and other lawmakers among the ancient Hebrews, before their religion had become corrupted. The philosophy of Epicurus as expressed in the poetry of Lucretius embodied these ideas, which had once been those of the Pythagoreans, the inventors of Greek geometry. They had understood the harmonic relationship between the sun and the planets, mediated by gravity, through the metaphor of Apollo and his lyre (see catalogue number 51). The correct form of human worship replicated this harmony in the structure of temples built around sacred fires (see catalogue numbers 15 and 62).

The arguments that Newton painstakingly developed in the viciously corrected draft that is on display also manifested themselves in other passages that he eventually sent to David Gregory. They show that Newton had certainly not abandoned the interpretation of his earlier drafts for Book III. Indeed, notes for this particular scholium appear in the interleaved copy of the *Principia* in which he was recording the changes to be made in the second edition (see catalogue number 43). Halley's awareness of Newton's concerns was reflected in his choice of Lucretius as the stylistic model for the ode that he composed for the first edition of the *Principia*. Although Newton did not in the end publish the 'classical scholia' to Book III of the *Principia*, David Gregory rehearsed the core of their arguments in the preface to his *Elementa astronomiae physicae et geometricae* (1702). He did not, however, mention his source.

It is important to realise that the ideas set out in the 'classical scholia' to Book III of the *Principia* do not constitute a version of the deism that perturbed English churchmen and moralists during the 1690s. The assimilation of primitive pagan religion to pristine Jewish and Christian teaching was orthodox enough in its assumptions, if not in the degree to which Newton carried the argument. There was no doubt in Newton's mind that the active and omnipresent God to whom he referred was also a being who intervened in human history, albeit normally through some sort of intermediary. The evidence for this came from the fulfilment of prophecy.

J.E. McGuire and P.M. Rattansi, 'Newton and the "Pipes of Pan"', *Notes and Records of the Royal Society of London*, 21 (1966), 108–143; Paolo Casini, 'Newton: The Classical Scholia', *History of Science*, 22 (1984), 1–58; I. Bernard Cohen, *Introduction to Newton's 'Principia'* (Cambridge, 1971), pp. 188–94.

Presented to Cambridge University Library by the fifth Earl of Portsmouth. See *A Catalogue of the Portsmouth Collection of Books and Papers written by or belonging to Sir Isaac Newton* (Cambridge, 1888), pp. 4–5.

57 *The Holy Bible*
(London, 1660)
(figure 35)
8°: A-2M^{8}, 2N^{2}; A-H^{8}; 2N^{3}-3A^{4}
16 × 10.5 cm
Trinity College, Cambridge, shelfmark Adv.d.1.10

Newton had begun to study the Bible in earnest during the 1670s, when the issue of having to take holy orders had seemed pressing. His temperament and upbringing convinced him to read the text in a strongly literalist manner and to pay particular attention to biblical prophecy. This was an area of study that contemporary lay people were urged to avoid because of its complexity and the danger of falling into error as a result of misunderstanding. Undeterred, Newton developed a method for the interpretation of prophecy based on the writings of the early seventeenth-century Cambridge divine, Joseph Mede. Mede's views were widely accepted and the scheme that Newton propounded to bring consistency to the unravelling of prophetic symbolism was not in itself controversial. As his skill as an interpreter developed, however, Newton's biblical criticism became more overtly unusual.

Its development took two principal forms. The first, which was undoubtedly present in Newton's earlier theological work but became particularly apparent in his writing from the late 1680s or early 1690s, was a close interest in finding prophetic and historical references to the Arian controversy of the fourth century (see catalogue number 59). This was a natural enough consequence of Newton's doubts about the scriptural and historical basis for the doctrine of the Trinity, which nevertheless seems to have become more pressing in the context of the struggle with Catholicism in England during the 1680s (see catalogue number 17) and the European war between Protestant and Catholic powers in the 1690s. Newton's anxieties about the exercise of the power of the Church over the individual conscience had long made him a sympathiser with Arius and his followers, who denied that Christ or the Holy Spirit were truly divine. To Newton, the growth and spread of Catholicism, and the multiplication of spiritual errors that he attributed to it, had their origins in the persecution of Arius. The undermining of Christianity that this represented was a defining example of the recurrent corruption of the pure, original religion of mankind that Newton had started to explore during the mid-1680s. Furthermore, like the rediscovery of the truth about ancient philosophy, the recovery of pure Christianity promised to support the arguments of Newton's natural philosophy.

The second change in the emphasis of Newton's theological writing also took place at the start of the 1690s. It took the form of an increasingly precise regard for the text of the Bible as it had been transmitted historically. Newton argued that scripture had been corrupted in order to justify the doctrines of Arius' opponents. An interest in the meaning and implication of the words of the Bible had been one of the earliest aspects of Newton's theology in the 1670s. Then he had been convinced by the implications of his reading to make a thorough investigation of the historical understanding of particular scriptural passages. The historical reconstruction of the transmission of parts of that text, however, only became an obsession in Newton's writing some twenty years later. Despite these developments, the whole of Newton's theological work drew on conclusions and assumptions that he had made early in his life. One of these was that it should be 'a duty of the greatest moment' to 'search the scriptures thyself... by frequent reading and constant meditation'.

The Bible on display was owned by Newton and bears witness to many of his theological concerns. It also indicates the importance of a relatively small number of works by contemporary interpreters that Newton felt were particularly worthy of note. Thus, the passages in the Old Testament that Newton marked by turning down page corners refer extensively to the doctrines of the primitive religion of Noah and to Jewish legal and religious development. They also draw attention to the detail of the prophecies of Daniel that Newton read in conjunction with the Book of Revelation from the New Testament. Passages that Newton noted in the New Testament relate partly to difficulties with the text of the Gospels as well as to descriptions of the nature of God in the letters of Paul. One of the most heavily annotated parts of this Bible was the Book of Revelation (sig. 2Z6r-7r on display, see figure 35). At the foot of the left hand page, Newton has included a reference to a discussion of Revelation 2:22 in Sir Norton Knatchbull's *Annotations upon Some Difficult Texts in all the Books of the New Testament* (Cambridge, 1693). Knatchbull was one of the authors whose interpretations Newton found interesting. Newton noted references to and sometimes disagreements from Knatchbull's alternative translation of individual New Testament verses on many pages of this Bible. The written annotations in this copy of the Bible relate largely to the translation and structure of the text and may well have been composed during the 1690s.

This is one of numerous Bibles that Newton owned. He possessed vernacular translations into English and French, editions in the original languages of Hebrew and Greek, many Latin translations, and polyglot compilations of versions that were held to be important for establishing the true text of scripture. The appearance of this particular Bible also suggests more than a purely scholarly interest in the book. It is a Bible designed for personal devotion, either in Church or at home, bound with the Book of Common Prayer and the Metrical Psalms. The binding in gold-tooled green morocco with gilded edges to the pages again indicates that it was intended for something other than a don's bookcase when it was purchased.

John Harrison, *The Library of Isaac Newton* (Cambridge, 1978), pp. 101–4, 173; Jewish National and University Library, Jerusalem, Ms. Yahuda 1.

Presented to Trinity College by John Cox, July 1878. According to his uncle, Joseph Cox of Hurstborne Priors, 'the Bible… was in the possession of my father-in-law Mr Edward Golding… His statement respecting it was that it was given by Sir Isaac Newton in his last illness to the woman who nursed him — it was given either by her or some member of her family to Mr Golding's mother…'

58 KING'S COLLEGE, CAMBRIDGE, KEYNES MS. 5, f. 138v

31 × 19.2 cm

This is a typical page from one of the numerous manuscripts that Newton wrote to set out the historical interpretation of prophecy. From the 1670s, he emulated Joseph Mede's method of comparing the prophecies of Daniel and Revelation and combining them to tell a single, chronological story that could be checked and dated by its apparent fulfilment in the events of human history. The opening pages of this manuscript, entitled 'The First Book Concerning the Language of the Prophets', probably date from the 1690s, although subsequent chapters of the work appear to have been written rather later, perhaps after 1700. The manuscript as a whole provides a chronological reading of the prophecies in Daniel and in Revelation with reference to the history of the Roman Empire and its successors. This was a subject that Newton had first written about in the 1670s. It occupied him in one way or another for much of the rest of his life.

In the part of the manuscript that is on display, Newton employed a chronological framework drawn from Revelation 8–11 that he interpreted in the light of Daniel 12. He concluded an analysis of the spread of Islam and the rise of the Turks by commenting: 'I leave it to be decided by time, whether the Turkish Empire come to its end before the sounding of the seventh Angel, or whether we are only to understand that its last hostile act against the Catholicks will be over at the fall of the tenth part of the great city or soon after, but the Empire it self not ruined before the sounding of the seventh Angel.' Newton argued that the punishments that God sent against the corrupted Christian Church would culminate in the delivery of the righteous by the return of the Messiah. He chose to describe this figure in the terms of the Old Testament, as 'Michael... that great Prince of Israel whom Daniel calls ~~Messiah~~ the anointed Prince', rather than in an overtly Christological manner. He also described the first resurrection of the elect and the subsequent restoration of the true worship of God on earth. Then he turned to the question of the timing of these apocalyptic events, arguing that the period specified by Daniel's 'numbers relating to [the] time of the end... [seems] to me to begin either with that time [AD] 609 or perhaps a little later.' When Newton wrote these words, he was arguing that the time from the utter corruption of Christianity by Trinitarians and Catholics and the establishment of the power of the Papacy until the restoration of the primitive religion might cover the period from the beginning of the seventh century to the year 1900. But he remained cautious over the beginning of Daniel's chronology, suggesting that Eastern Christendom resisted idolatry for longer than the West, perhaps until 841 AD. The return of the Messiah might thus be delayed by a corresponding period.

Newton's interpretation of prophecy was intimately linked to his sense of the indivisible and omnipotent nature of God the Father and his denial of Christ's divinity. These beliefs helped to determine the history of the corruption of religion that he identified. That history itself depended on the characterisation of primitive religion that Newton had drawn up in the 1680s. Newton's Arianism was even apparent in the manner in which he chose to express the dates in his chronology. Occasionally his pen slipped, for example once in this manuscript when he wrote the date 'AD 841'. He quickly corrected this error to 'AC 841', thus using a notation that was common among his contemporaries but which for him had additional meaning. In Newton's eyes, the historical Christ was certainly a special figure, sent by God, and after his birth the world had indeed been changed. But only God the Father could be called 'Lord' without risk of idolatry (see catalogue number 60).

Sotheby sale, 14 July 1936, lot 242; purchased by Maggs Brothers for £170. Offered to J.M. Keynes for a twenty percent commission on 30 July 1936.

59 KING'S COLLEGE, CAMBRIDGE, KEYNES MS. 10/1, F. 1r
29 × 18 cm

During the late 1680s and early 1690s, Newton reformulated his interpretation of the corruption of the Christian Church. He began to concentrate more closely on the historical figures involved in the early Church's adoption of the doctrine of the Trinity and to try to work out what was said about them, particularly in the writings of the Church Fathers. The two individuals on whom Newton focussed his attention most clearly were the theologians Arius and Athanasius. Arius (d. 336) was the champion of the position that Christ – though not simply a man – was subordinate to God the Father and had been created by him at the beginning of time. Athanasius (c. 296–373) was bishop of Alexandria from 328. He was largely responsible for the condemnation of Arius at the Council of Nicaea in 325 and subsequently refused to receive him back into communion in Alexandria.

Newton had access to abundant, if highly contradictory, material about both of these men in the writings of the Church Fathers, including Athanasius himself, and the historians of the early Church. Most of the relevant sources had originally been written in Greek, but Newton seems largely to have worked from translations and editions made by his contemporaries in Latin. He teased out an account of the actions and beliefs of Arius and Athanasius that ran against the grain of most previous historical writing about the Arian controversy. In a long manuscript entitled 'Paradoxical Questions concerning the morals & actions of Athanasius & his followers', he vilified Athanasius' behaviour and cast doubt on the negative remarks made by historians about Arius. He tried to show that the beliefs of the Arians had been those of true Christians before the Council of Nicaea. In Newton's eyes, the short-lived persecution of the Athanasians by the Emperor testified to their sinfulness as well as their heresy. Newton praised the later actions of the Arian kings of the Vandals and the Goths both for their punishment of Athanasian immorality and for their tolerance of genuine religious belief. The significant dates identified through this historical work also helped Newton to clarify the interpretation of the events described in prophecy. He argued that the triumph of idolatry in the Christian Church, represented by the success of Trinitarian doctrine, was one of the principal subjects described in the visions given in Daniel and in Revelation.

The main target of Newton's criticism throughout his historical writing was the Catholic Church, which, he argued, had added the idolatrous worship of saints and the tyranny of Papal power to the errors of Trinitarianism. In a number of manuscripts, he suggested that whereas Catholicism should be uprooted, toleration was appropriate for other Christians who shared the fundamentals of the true faith. He appears to have believed that the doctrine of the Church of England could one day be made compatible with those fundamentals, although he was careful not to reveal the full extent of his heretical ideas beyond a narrow circle of friends. Nevertheless, Newton's theological conclusions were ultimately incompatible with those of the Church in which he was born and would die.

William Andrews Clark Memorial Library, Los Angeles, Newton Ms. 'Paradoxical Questions'; Fondation Martin Bodmer, Geneva, Newton Ms. 'Of the Church'; Maurice Wiles, *Archetypal Heresy* (Oxford, 1996); Alan E. Shapiro, 'Beyond the Dating Game: Watermark Clusters and the Composition of Newton's *Opticks*', in P.M. Harman and Alan E. Shapiro (eds), *The Investigation of Difficult Things* (Cambridge, 1992), pp. 181–227.

Sotheby sale, 14 July 1936, lot 268; purchased by J.M. Keynes for £34.

60 ISAAC NEWTON, *Philosophiae naturalis principia mathematica*
2nd edition (Cambridge, 1713)
(figure 36)
4°: a-c^4, D^2, B-3Q^4, 3R^2
19.2 × 12.6 cm
Cambridge University Library, shelfmark Adv. b. 39.2

During the 1690s, Newton seemed set on the production both of a new edition of the *Principia* and of some contribution to public debate about the status of the doctrine of the Trinity. Several of his friends published books that hinted at the direction of Newton's scholarly activity. Yet, in the end, Newton remained silent. The text of the *Opticks*, in particular the additional queries included in the Latin edition of 1706 (see catalogue numbers 29 and 30), reflected in many ways his continuing puzzlement concerning any physical mechanism that might lie behind the effects of gravity, magnetism and chemical transmutation, as well as the behaviour of light. The solutions that Newton had advanced in the *Opticks*, although they indicated further shifts in his thinking, also provoked controversy, as did the publications of several of his disciples, notably William Whiston. Furthermore, despite the efforts of David Gregory, it appeared that the second edition of the *Principia* was running into the sand.

It seems that material concerns, as much as anything else, finally brought a second edition of the *Principia* to the press. Richard Bentley, who had been one of the first serious expositors of the *Principia* in the early 1690s, noticed that copies of the work were becoming increasing hard to find and fetched a high price. In the mid-1690s, Bentley had been instrumental in the establishment of the University Press in Cambridge under the direction of the Vice-Chancellor. Despite its considerable scholarly achievements, the new Press was not a financial success and Bentley and his collaborators remained on the lookout for suitable books that might turn a small profit. A second edition of the *Principia* appeared to be one of these. In 1708, Bentley persuaded Newton to allow him to prepare a specimen for this publication at the Cambridge University Press. He had already managed to talk Newton into permitting Whiston to edit and print a manuscript of his lectures on algebra, supposedly delivered in the 1670s and early 1680s. He was now able to offer Newton freedom from the concerns that perhaps most bothered him about a new edition of his most important work: the trouble of finding suitable printers and the cost in terms of time of correcting and seeing the book through the press. Bentley was well aware of the difficulty that English compositors had in setting complex Latin texts and of the extra demands that this might impose on the author. At first, he proposed to look after the production of the *Principia* himself, but as its demands became more complicated he abandoned the work. He recommended, however, that Roger Cotes (see catalogue number 37) should supervise the edition for Newton. The result was a collaboration that substantially improved the text of the *Principia*, despite the delays that were introduced by the realisation that several parts of Book III in particular needed further consideration.

On 6 January 1713, Newton wrote to Cotes to send him some final corrected calculations and warn him about two possible additions to the second edition of the *Principia*, which was already all but printed off. One of these was a proposed appendix on 'the attraction of the small particles of bodies', worrying away further at the problems that Newton had tried to solve in previous, rejected scholia (see catalogue number 56); the other was 'a Scholium of about a quarter of a Sheet to be added to the [end] of the book'. Newton never completed the appendix that he mentioned. It almost certainly would have contained a discussion of an electrical spirit through which he now believed 'the particles of bodies mutually draw one another together at short distances'. These were ideas that he would develop in the changes that he made to the second edition of the *Opticks* in 1717. The other addition that Newton proposed fared better. This was the General Scholium that he sent to Cotes on 2 March 1713. It discussed the broader cosmological implications of the action of gravity and included a final paragraph that mentioned Newton's theories about an electrical spirit.

The General Scholium argued that the ordered and unified system of the heavens that Newton had described in the *Principia* testified to creation and government by an all-powerful God. In this passage, Newton surprisingly reintroduced some of the evidence that he had been considering in the 1690s, in the form of a footnote to biblical and classical references that supported his account of the nature of God (see p. 483 on display and figure 36). That account was a strange one. It stressed the power and independence of God and suggested that he was defined by lordship and by the dominion that he held over the whole of his creation: 'For God is a relative word and refers to servants: & divinity

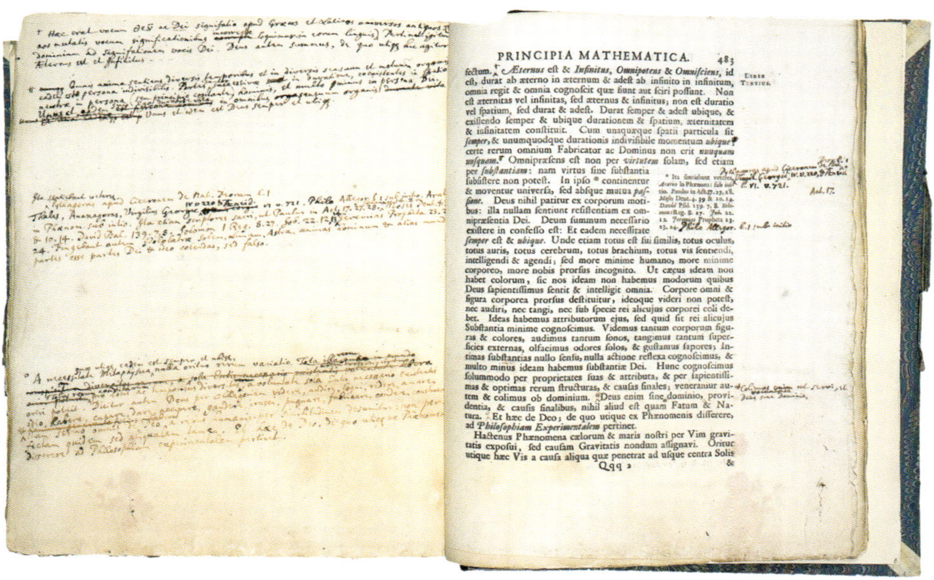

PRINCIPIA MATHEMATICA. 483

ſectum. Æternus eſt & *Infinitus*, *Omnipotens* & *Omniſciens*, id eſt, durat ab æterno in æternum & adeſt ab infinito in infinitum, omnia regit & omnia cognoſcit quæ fiunt aut ſciri poſſunt. Non eſt æternitas vel infinitas, ſed æternus & infinitus; non eſt duratio vel ſpatium, ſed durat & adeſt. Durat ſemper & adeſt ubique, & exiſtendo ſemper & ubique durationem & ſpatium, æternitatem & infinitatem conſtituit. Cum unaquæque ſpatii particula ſit *ſemper*, & unumquodque durationis indiviſibile momentum *ubique*, certe rerum omnium Fabricator ac Dominus non erit *nunquam nuſquam*. Omnipræſens eſt non per *virtutem* ſolam, sed etiam per *ſubſtantiam*: nam virtus ſine ſubſtantia ſubſiſtere non poteſt. In ipſo * continentur & moventur univerſa, ſed abſque mutua *paſſione*. Deus nihil patitur ex corporum motibus: illa nullam ſentiunt reſiſtentiam ex omnipræſentia Dei. Deum ſummum neceſſario exiſtere in confeſſo eſt: Et eadem neceſſitate *ſemper* eſt & *ubique*. Unde etiam totus eſt ſui ſimilis, totus oculus, totus auris, totus cerebrum, totus brachium, totus vis ſentiendi, intelligendi & agendi; ſed more minime humano, more minime corporeo, more nobis prorſus incognito. Ut cæcus ideam non habet colorum, ſic nos ideam non habemus modorum quibus Deus ſapientiſſimus ſentit & intelligit omnia. Corpore omni & figura corporea prorſus deſtituitur, ideoque videri non poteſt, nec audiri, nec tangi, nec ſub ſpecie rei alicujus corporei coli debet. Ideas habemus attributorum ejus, ſed quid ſit rei alicujus Subſtantia minime cognoſcimus. Videmus tantum corporum figuras & colores, audimus tantum ſonos, tangimus tantum ſuperficies externas, olfacimus odores ſolos, & guſtamus ſapores; Intimas ſubſtantias nullo ſenſu, nulla actione reflexa cognoſcimus, & multo minus ideam habemus ſubſtantiæ Dei. Hunc cognoſcimus ſolummodo per proprietates ſuas & attributa, & per ſapientiſſimas & optimas rerum ſtructuras, & cauſas finales; veneramur autem & colimus ob dominium. Deus enim ſine dominio, providentia, & cauſis finalibus, nihil aliud eſt quam Fatum & Natura. Et hæc de Deo; de quo utique ex Phænomenis diſſerere, ad *Philoſophiam Experimentalem* pertinet.

Haſtenus Phænomena cælorum & maris noſtri per Vim gravitatis expoſui, ſed cauſam Gravitatis nondum aſſignavi. Oritur utique hæc Vis a cauſa aliqua quæ penetrat ad uſque centra Solis &

Qqq 2

LIBER TERTIUS.

* Ita ſentiebant veteres, *Aratus* in Phænomenis ſub initio. *Paulus* in Act. 17. 27, 28. *Moſes* Deut. 4. 39 & 10. 14. *David* Pſal. 139. 7, 8. *Solomon* 1 Reg. 8. 27. *Job* 22. 12. *Jeremias* Propheta 23. 23, 24.

FIGURE 36
Describing God and his activity: additions and corrections to the General Scholium, University Library, shelfmark Adv. b. 39.2, p. 483.

is the absolute dominion of God, not over his own body… but over servants.' The terms that Newton used to describe God were unusual and reflected his covert Arian beliefs, in which Christ himself was a creature, subordinate to God. They echoed the language of a number of Socinian authors, who also denied the doctrine of the Trinity.

In 1712, Newton's close friend, Samuel Clarke, published his *Scripture Doctrine of the Trinity*. Clarke had translated Newton's *Opticks* into Latin and, from 1709, had been the rector of the London parish in which Newton lived. There, he was said to have modified the saying of the Creed, in order to take into account reservations about the doctrine of the Trinity that he shared with Newton. Clarke's book, which made public his doubts about the Trinity, caused an immediate furore at a time of considerable political uncertainty. It is just possible that the debate over *The Scripture Doctrine of the Trinity* encouraged Newton to be uncharacteristically bold in the clarification of his ideas in the General Scholium.

In the form in which Newton sent it to Cotes, the General Scholium occupied half of a sheet of paper (4 pages) when printed. Its extent had been determined in part by the layout of the rest of the text of the *Principia* and the plans that Cotes and Newton had made for its printing.

Unsurprisingly, Newton both revised and amplified the General Scholium in the third edition of the *Principia*. Some of his additions, for example the expansion of the list of classical authorities that supported the account of the nature of God, can be seen in the pages from his interleaved copy of the second edition that are on display (see figure 36).

D.F. McKenzie, *The Cambridge University Press 1696–1712*, 2 vols (Cambridge, 1966), vol. 1, 330–6; I. Bernard Cohen, *Introduction to Newton's 'Principia'* (Cambridge, 1971), pp. 239–45; Alexandre Koyré and I. Bernard Cohen (eds), *Isaac Newton's Philosophiae Naturalis Principia Mathematica*, 2 vols (Cambridge, 1972), vol. 2, 759–65; H. W. Turnbull, J.F. Scott, A.R. Hall and Laura Tilling (eds), *The Correspondence of Isaac Newton*, 7 vols (Cambridge, 1959–77), vol. 4, 518–20; vol. 5, 361–9; Larry Stewart, 'Seeing through the Scholium: Religion and Reading Newton in the Eighteenth Century', *History of Science*, 34 (1996), 123–65; Stephen D. Snobelen, 'Isaac Newton, Heretic: The Strategies of a Nicodemite', *British Journal for the History of Science*, 32 (1999), 381–419; John Harrison, *The Library of Isaac Newton* (Cambridge, 1978), p. 202.

Presented to Cambridge University Library by the fifth Earl of Portsmouth. See *A Catalogue of the Portsmouth Collection of Books and Papers written by or belonging to Sir Isaac Newton* (Cambridge, 1888), p. 47.

61 CAMBRIDGE UNIVERSITY LIBRARY, MS. ADD. 3965, f. 357r

30.5 × 18.6 cm

Cotes was dissatisfied with some aspects of the first version of the General Scholium, which was sent to him on 2 March 1713. Newton reworked the text in a number of drafts over the rest of the month. In the page on display, Newton has rearranged the opening passages of the General Scholium, numbering paragraphs to produce the sequence that later appeared in print.

A. Rupert Hall and Marie Boas Hall (eds), *Unpublished Scientific Papers of Isaac Newton* (Cambridge, 1962), pp. 348–64.

Presented to Cambridge University Library by the fifth Earl of Portsmouth. See *A Catalogue of the Portsmouth Collection of Books and Papers written by or belonging to Sir Isaac Newton* (Cambridge, 1888), pp. 4–5.

62 CAMBRIDGE UNIVERSITY LIBRARY, MS. ADD. 3988, f. 102r

(figure 37)

32 × 20.4 cm

The history of worship played a substantial role in almost all of Newton's theological writings. The correct form of worship had been

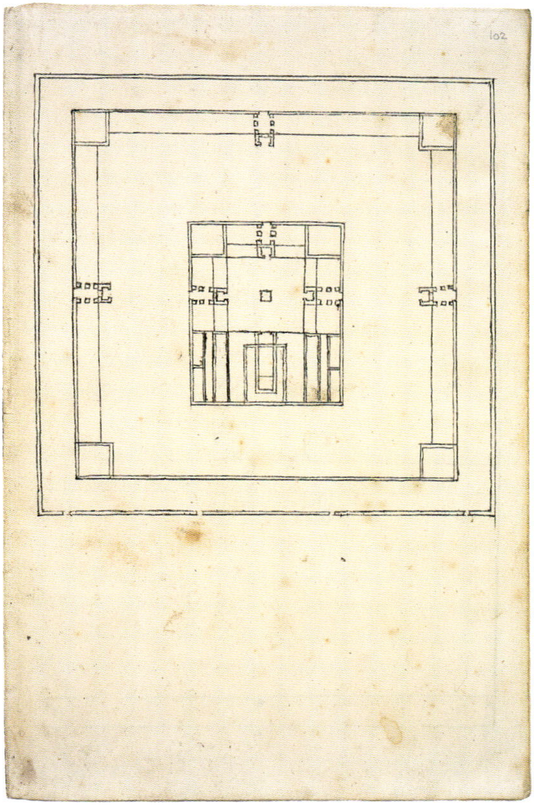

FIGURE 37
The ground-plan of the Temple of Solomon, from the manuscript of Newton's *Chronology of Ancient Kingdoms Amended* (published posthumously in 1728), University Library, Ms. Add. 3988, f. 102r.

established by the patriarchs and was preserved for a time among both Jews and Gentiles. The history of its corruption was one of the major themes of Newton's interpretation of prophecy. Within that history, the idolatry of the Athanasians and their Catholic successors had a special place of infamy. Newton began to investigate the history of worship in the 1670s. The study of the building and liturgy of the Temple of Jerusalem was particularly important for his exposition of the Book of Revelation, in which the Temple was the setting for the unveiling of prophecy. Newton's understanding of the Temple and its cult was transformed by his reading of Maimonides (see catalogue number 15) and other Jewish sources, probably in the early 1680s.

Newton made several attempts to reconstruct the appearance of the Temple. Of necessity, these were based largely on the account given in

Ezekiel. They also drew heavily on earlier interpretations of this biblical text, especially those printed in the prolegomena to the London polyglot Bible, which Newton owned. Newton's task was made harder by the problem of determining the length of the ancient Hebrew cubit, the measure used in Ezekiel's description of the Temple.

The plan of the Temple of Solomon that is on display (figure 37) is taken from the manuscript used in the publication of Newton's *Chronology of Ancient Kingdoms Amended* (see catalogue number 63). It shows the Temple itself and the Court of Priests that surrounded it, both of which are enclosed by the larger Court of the People, around which a pavement runs on three sides.

Similar drawings by Newton (formerly in the library of Babson College, Wellesley, Massachusetts, Ms. 434) may be found in the Dibner Library at the Massachusetts Institute of Technology.

Presented to Cambridge University Library by the fifth Earl of Portsmouth. See *A Catalogue of the Portsmouth Collection of Books and Papers written by or belonging to Sir Isaac Newton* (Cambridge, 1888), p. 47.

63 CAMBRIDGE UNIVERSITY LIBRARY, MS. ADD. 3988, BINDING *(figure 38)*

Newton's *Chronology* appeared in 1728, the year after his death, and was edited by John Conduitt (1688–1737). Conduitt had married Newton's niece in 1717 and acted as executor for the estate. He posted a bond to cover Newton's expenses at the Mint, where he succeeded Newton as Master. Newton left no will when he died on 20 March 1727. In return for his expenses, Conduitt received Newton's manuscripts, although he had to cede any profits that might result from publication to be divided among the heirs. Newton's papers were appraised for probate on 18 April and subsequently moved to Conduitt's house in London. Thomas Pellet, a fellow of the Royal Society, drew up an inventory of the manuscripts in May and then tried to determine what might be suitable for publication. He decided that five titles might be candidates for the press, of which three were successfully sold to booksellers and prepared for publication over the next few years. Conduitt had the manuscripts of these three books bound specially (see figure 38) but otherwise seemed largely unconcerned about the appearance of Newton's papers.

It was not surprising that the papers that made up the *Chronology of Ancient Kingdoms Amended* should have been among the unpublished

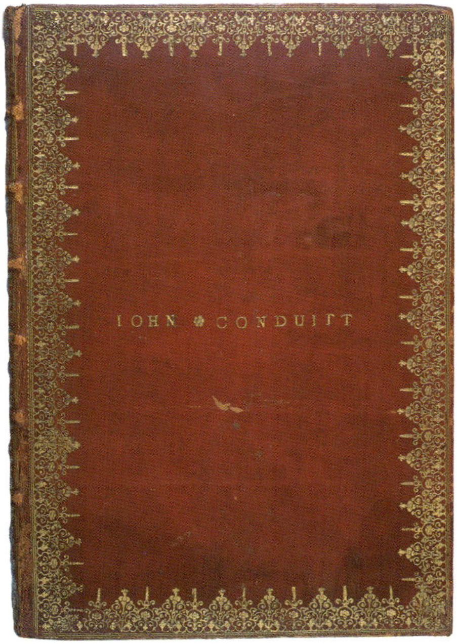

38

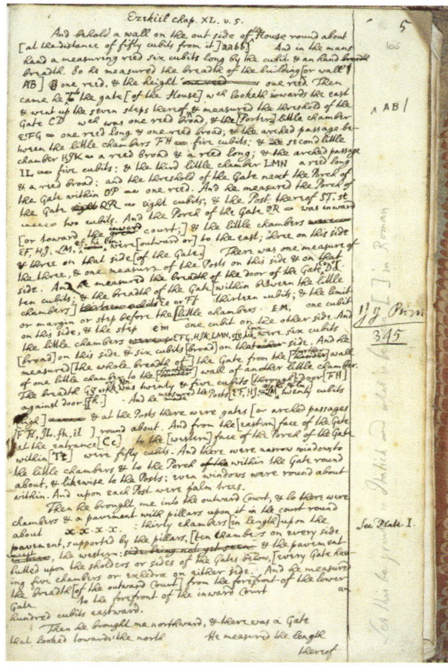
Ezekiel chap. XL. v. 5.

39

FIGURE 38
The manuscript of Newton's *Chronology* bound for his executor, John Conduitt, University Library, Ms. Add. 3988, binding.

FIGURE 39
Editing Newton's unpublished theological manuscripts for publication, University Library, Ms. Add. 3988, f. 106r.

works by Newton that found a buyer after his death. Newton himself had been preparing his chronology for the press when he died. His decision to undertake this work was prompted by the publication in Paris in 1725 of a pirated edition of one of his historical manuscripts. After Newton's death, a text was established by Conduitt with the assistance of Pellet and Martin Folkes (see figure 39). Conduitt successfully obtained permission to dedicate the work to Queen Caroline, who had discussed it with Newton several years before in an interview that led indirectly to the Parisian piracy of part of its text. The printed *Chronology* was not, however, a success. Despite the inclusion of a chapter discussing the Temple of Solomon, most of the work was based around an attempt to redate the history of the Greek, Egyptian, Assyrian, Babylonian and Persian empires. Newton ingeniously compared differing historical records and deployed astronomical as well as calendrical evidence to draw up a new chronology for the ancient world. Unfortunately, the material that Newton had been preparing to publish was deliberately shorn of most of its context in the history of ancient religion.

In April 1727, James West, an observer at Newton's funeral in Westminster Abbey, informed the Oxford scholar Thomas Hearne that Newton's *Chronology* 'was near finished... It is very short and I am told, will be a Diminution of his Learning if ever it appears.' Although the printed *Chronology* was longer than West had expected, it sold sufficiently poorly to mean that its publishers, who had paid the massive sum of £350 for the work, still had copies on their hands over forty years later. A second edition, really a reissue, was published in 1770. Rather pathetically, this was printed alongside some scholarly correspondence that discussed possible explanations for the deficiencies of the book. Here it was noted that abundant drafts and relevant papers had existed in Newton's study and that he had worked on the subject of the book for many years, altering and abbreviating what he had written. The writer of one letter, Zachary Pearce, who had visited Newton in 1725 or 1726 while he was editing the *Chronology*, suggested that 'It is a pity, that he took so much of the same method in his Chronology which he took in his *Principia*, &c; concealing his proofs, and leaving it to the sagacity of others to discover them.'

Frank E. Manuel, *Isaac Newton. Historian* (Cambridge, 1963); D.T. Whiteside (ed.), *The Mathematical Papers of Isaac Newton*, 8 vols (Cambridge, 1967–81), vol. 1, xvii–xx; Rob Iliffe, 'A "Connected System"? The Snare of a Beautiful Hand and the Unity of Newton's Archive', in Michael Hunter (ed.), *Archives of the Scientific Revolution* (Woodbridge, 1998), pp. 137–57; Cambridge University Library, Mss. Add. 3987–90; Bodleian Library, Oxford, Ms. Rawlinson Letters 11, number 121.

FOOTPRINTS OF THE LION

Newton died, covered with honours, in 1727 and was buried grandly in Westminster Abbey. He had become President of the Royal Society in 1703 and was knighted in 1705. As Master of the Mint from 1699, he was a wealthy and successful servant of the state. Yet, as Newton's heirs investigated the books and manuscripts that remained after his death, it became increasingly apparent that the outward face of genius was quite different from the private life of an alchemist and heretic who had, for much of his life, deliberately avoided publicity of any kind. Newton's books were sold and few of his papers were deemed worthy of publication. His heirs and their descendants guarded the rest of them closely. The transfer of the Portsmouth papers to Cambridge University in 1872 opened up the possibility of studying Newton's scientific development, as it was then conceived. In 1936, the 'personal' papers that had been returned to the family were sold at auction in order to meet death duties and other family expenses. The economist, John Maynard Keynes, bought many of them and subsequently formed the view that Newton was 'the last of the magicians'. The study of the traces that Newton had left in the pages of his manuscripts began in earnest after 1945. It continues today around the world. With the University Library's acquisition of the Macclesfield Collection, letters and papers that were preserved by friends and disciples of Newton have been reunited for the first time since their creation with others that were kept by his family.

64 IVORY BUST OF SIR ISAAC NEWTON
23.8 × 15 cm

R.J.E. Hanson presented this copy of a bust of Newton by David Le Marchand to Cambridge University Library in 1936. The original was sculpted in 1718 and was one of several representations of Newton by Le Marchand.

65 CAMBRIDGE UNIVERSITY LIBRARY, MS. ADD. 3960(2), p. 1
23.6 × 18.6 cm

William Jones (see catalogue numbers 10 and 36) wrote this account of Newton's invention of the calculus in the 1730s. It drew heavily on his knowledge of Newton's own version of events and on the papers in his possession. Nevertheless it also contained a number of errors, including the date given in its opening line. It was communicated to Thomas Birch (1705–66), who was compiling a huge biographical dictionary in which extensive reference was made to the works of each subject. The entry in Birch's *A General Dictionary, Historical and Critical* (1734–41) was the first published biography of Newton by a British author.

D.T. Whiteside (ed.), *The Mathematical Papers of Isaac Newton*, 8 vols (Cambridge, 1967–81), vol. 8, xx–xxiii; A. Rupert Hall, *Isaac Newton. Eighteenth-Century Perspectives* (Oxford, 1999), pp. 75–95.

Presented to Cambridge University Library by the fifth Earl of Portsmouth. See *A Catalogue of the Portsmouth Collection of Books and Papers written by or belonging to Sir Isaac Newton* (Cambridge, 1888), p. 2.

66 NEWTON'S DEATH MASK
(figure 40)
20 × 14 × 8 cm
King's College, Cambridge

John Michael Rysbrack (1694–1770) was probably the artist who prepared this plaster death mask of Newton. Rysbrack was also the sculptor of the monument to Newton in Westminster Abbey (see catalogue number 67). Several copies of Newton's death mask were circulating among artists in the eighteenth century and a number survive. This one was bought by John Maynard Keynes at the Sotheby sale of Newton's manuscripts in 1936.

Michael Jaffe, *The European Fame of Isaac Newton* (Cambridge, 1974), pp. 23–4.

Sotheby sale, 14 July 1936, lot 332, purchased by J.M. Keynes for £34.

FIGURE 40
Newton's Death Mask by John Michael Rysbrack, King's College, Cambridge.

67 KING'S COLLEGE, CAMBRIDGE, MS. KEYNES 131/6
(figure 41)
22.4 × 17.7

After Newton's death, his body lay in state in Westminster Abbey on 28 March 1727 and was later buried in the nave. James West, who witnessed the proceedings, commented that 'People talk of a very magnificent Monument to be erected to him'. The sculptor Rysbrack prepared a sarcophagus that was unveiled in April 1731. It was based on designs that were drawn up by Conduitt. This drawing has been attributed to Conduitt and is slightly different from the monument that Rysbrack executed. Unlike that work, it bears the couplet that Alexander Pope composed in memory of Newton: 'All Nature & its Laws lay hid in night:/ God said, Let Newton be & all was light'.

Francis Haskell, 'The Apotheosis of Newton in Art', in Robert Palter (ed.), *The Annus Mirabilis of Sir Isaac Newton 1666–1966* (Cambridge, Mass., 1970), pp. 302–21; Bodleian Library, Oxford, Ms. Rawlinson Letters 11, number 121. Exhibited at the Fitzwilliam Museum, November 1973-January 1974: Michael Jaffe, *The European Fame of Isaac Newton* (Cambridge, 1974), p. 27.

Sotheby sale, 14 July 1936, lot 214, bought by Dawson's for £3. 10s.; subsequently acquired by J.M. Keynes.

FIGURE 41
A sketch for Newton's tomb, with proposed epitaphs by the poet, Alexander Pope, King's College, Cambridge, Keynes Ms. 131/6 .

68 *A Catalogue of the Portsmouth Collection of Books and Papers written by or belonging to Sir Isaac Newton*
(Cambridge, 1888)
17.2 × 10 cm
Cambridge University Library, shelfmark A122.2.105

Thomas Pellet decided that almost all of the manuscripts that he assessed on behalf of Newton's heirs were 'not fit to be printed' (see catalogue number 63). Despite the financial disappointment that this implied, Conduitt and others were probably not surprised by this outcome. The bulk of Newton's unpublished papers consisted either of drafts for works that had already been published or of manuscripts whose content seemed likely to tarnish the reputation for genius that Newton had already acquired. In any case, neither the *Chronology* nor an edition of some of Newton's writings about Daniel and Revelation, *Observations upon the Prophecies* (1733) experienced startling success once they had appeared in print. Despite their incoherence, both of these books managed to generate a considerable amount of criticism, particularly from readers who began to suspect that Newton's arguments led to heretical conclusions from which they were being kept by sleight of hand. Moreover the terms of Conduitt's arrangement with Newton's other heirs gave him a greater interest in keeping any manuscripts out of the sight of possible pirates than in securing their publication himself.

In 1755, some chronological and theological manuscripts were nevertheless sent to Arthur Ashley Sykes, who sympathised with Newton's religious ideas, with a view to publication. Most of these in fact related to work that had already appeared in print in some form. They were not published, but when Sykes died a few years later they were also not returned to Newton's family. In the 1770s, when he was preparing an edition of Newton's *Opera Omnia*, Samuel Horsley had access briefly to the rest of Newton's manuscripts at Hurstbourne Park, the home of the Earls of Portsmouth into whose family Conduitt's daughter had married. Sir David Brewster published a few passages from these papers in the revised edition of his biography of Newton that appeared in 1855.

Concern that Newton's papers might not be safe at Hurstbourne Park seems to have encouraged the fifth Earl of Portsmouth, Isaac Newton Wallop, to seek the advice of Cambridge University. The University sent the astronomer, John Couch Adams, and the mathematician and physicist, George Stokes, to examine Newton's archive. In August 1872, the Earl of Portsmouth offered to lend Newton's papers to Cambridge, so that they could 'be carefully investigated to see whether they relate to, or are rough drafts of his works.' He also decided that 'in the event of their proving to be the calculations from which [Newton] made his deductions in his works, I am willing then to make them over to the University.' A Syndicate was now established to assess Newton's manuscripts. Adams and Stokes were largely responsible for considering the mathematical and scientific papers. The University Registrary, H.R. Luard, who checked much of Newton's correspondence, and G.D. Liveing, who catalogued the alchemical manuscripts, assisted them in their work. After sixteen years, these four men succeeded in preparing a catalogue of the Portsmouth collection, including both the manuscripts that were now donated to the University Library and those that had to be returned to the family. The 'heirlooms' that the Earl of Portsmouth retained consisted of the majority of Newton's 'non-scientific' alchemical and theological papers together with many personal items, including much correspondence and Newton's papers from the Mint. One of the main activities of the Syndicate had been to supervise the transcription of many of those letters.

The published catalogue of the Portsmouth Collection leaves much to be desired. Its entries are very brief and often misleading and its editors did not always take very much trouble over their task. Nevertheless, in 1888, the University Library became by far the most important public collection of Newton manuscripts.

Rob Iliffe, 'A "Connected System"? The Snare of a Beautiful Hand and the Unity of Newton's Archive', in Michael Hunter (ed.), *Archives of the Scientific Revolution* (Woodbridge, 1998), pp. 137–57; D.T. Whiteside (ed.), *The Mathematical Papers of Isaac Newton*, 8 vols (Cambridge, 1967–81), vol. 1, xvii–xxxiii; Cambridge University Library, Mss. Add. 2588, ff. 6–11, 494–6; 7656, numbers A158, 167.

69 KING'S COLLEGE, CAMBRIDGE, MS. PP/59/9–10
(Sotheby & Co., *Catalogue of the Newton Papers sold by order of the Viscount Lymington* (London, 1936), pp. 4–5)
18.5 × 11 cm

Under the strain of death duties and of the expenses of a family divorce, Viscount Lymington, the Trustee of the Portsmouth Estates, decided to sell the Newton papers that remained in the family's possession. In

March 1936, they were delivered to Sotheby's in New Bond Street, where they were catalogued by John Cameron Taylor for auction on 13 and 14 July. The Sotheby sale was a major event for booksellers but attracted scarcely any interest from institutions. The causes of this are hard to fathom but may relate to the international situation, the sense that Cambridge already possessed all that mattered of Newton's papers, fatigue in a market that was already awash with books from Newton's library (see catalogue number 71), or even disquiet at Lord Lymington's right-wing political views. However, if libraries had hoped to pick up selected items with little trouble from future booksellers' catalogues, they were largely disappointed by the efforts of individuals. Lord Wakefield bought Newton's administrative papers from the New York dealer, Gabriel Wells, who had purchased the huge lot containing them at Sotheby's. He later donated them to the Mint. Much of the rest of the history of the manuscripts dispersed at the Sotheby sale can be expressed as a contest between two men, John Maynard Keynes (1893–1946) and Abraham Shalom Ezekiel Yahuda (1877–1951) (see catalogue number 70).

Keynes, who came from a prosperous Cambridge family, had made his name as an economist and gathered a fortune on the stock market. He had been collecting early printed books since he was an undergraduate. He had bought one or two items from Newton's library from the Guildford bookseller, Thomas Thorp, in the early 1920s and had acquired a copy of the first edition of the *Principia* as recently as 30 May 1936. On 15 July 1936, the day after the sale, he wrote that 'I have been up here for the last two days spending many hours in the auction rooms at the dispersal of the papers of Sir Isaac Newton... They went, as it seems to me, extraordinarily reasonably, and I think I have bought almost everything which ought to remain in Cambridge... Among other things I bought Sir Isaac's Death Mask, which is extraordinarily interesting' (see catalogue number 66).

Keynes' initial confidence in his purchases soon dissipated, however, as he decided that rather than simply cherry picking, he should make a serious collection of Newton's manuscripts, especially the alchemical papers in which he had shown no special interest at the sale. He therefore followed up the records of purchasers and prices that he had carefully made at the time of the sale. On 3 August he contacted the London bookseller Ernest Maggs, who had purchased more lots than anyone else, informing him that he had decided 'to form a very substantial collection of these papers with the idea of keeping them permanently in Cambridge'. When he wrote to Gabriel Wells on 8 September, Keynes apologised: 'I am sorry to have been too late with some of the others, but it is my own fault. I only gradually came to the decision to make my collection comprehensive. It is also only gradually that I came to the view that the papers concerning alchemy were really interesting.'

Pages from Keynes' marked up copy of the sale catalogue bear his later comments out. They record his first purchases at the sale (from which he came away with thirty-nine lots in total). They also note the fate of many lots (for example lot 32, for which see catalogue number 52) that he did not buy then but acquired later from booksellers, usually at very modest rates for commission. Keynes ringed the numbers of the lots that subsequently entered his collection in this way. But there were other lots, for example numbers 22 and 28 that Keynes rejected entirely or in part when dealers offered them to him. The collection that he was building was not an indiscriminate one, and it was shaped at all times by his own changing vision of its purpose.

P. E. Spargo, 'Sotheby's, Keynes and Yahuda — the 1936 Sale of Newton's Manuscripts', in P.M. Harman and Alan E. Shapiro (eds), *The Investigation of Difficult Things* (Cambridge, 1992), pp. 115–34; David Scrase and Peter Croft, *Maynard Keynes. Collector of Pictures, Books and Manuscripts* (Cambridge, 1983); A.N.L. Munby, *Essays and Papers*,ed. Nicolas Barker (London, 1977), pp. 19–26; King's College, Cambridge, Mss. PP58–9.

70 KING'S COLLEGE, CAMBRIDGE, MS. PP/58/186
25.7 × 20.3 cm

By the time that Keynes was buying up Newton manuscripts from the booksellers, someone else had begun to take a close interest in the sale. This was A.S. Yahuda, an émigré Jewish scholar, who was a serious collector of oriental manuscripts. At the beginning of August 1936, Yahuda first approached the New York dealer, Gabriel Wells, who had spent more money than anyone else at Sotheby's in order to acquire twenty-three substantial lots. Yahuda was able to buy a number of mainly theological manuscripts from Wells and was soon treading on Keynes' toes. By September, the two men were in correspondence and embarked on an exchange both of manuscripts and of ideas. There is little doubt that Keynes regarded Yahuda's intrusion on his collecting as a nuisance, but he nevertheless collaborated with him in order to improve the coherence of his own group of manuscripts. Yahuda, for his part, was astonishingly successful at building up a substantial collection of Newton's theological papers, despite having had no representative at the Sotheby sale. One area in which Keynes sought Yahuda's help quite genuinely was in the interpretation of the manuscripts that he had acquired. In the letter on display, from 3 April 1938, Keynes discussed the credentials of a potential cataloguer of his manuscripts whom Yahuda had recommended. In the process he revealed a great deal about the development of his own interest in his collection: 'What is it Newton really thought he was doing? Is it all the usual stuff and nonsense? Or is there some glimmering of the beginnings of genuine chemistry?'

This letter marked the start of Keynes' final falling out with Yahuda, whom he already suspected (with some justice) of purloining one of his alchemical manuscripts during a swap. Keynes was particularly concerned to identify Yahuda's intentions for his manuscripts. Yahuda had already hinted that others were involved in his collecting activities and it gradually dawned on Keynes that he might be part of 'a syndicate which hoped to sell [Newton's papers] at a high price'.

Keynes' judgement was both correct and unfair. Certainly Yahuda and his partners did try to sell their collection to a number of major American libraries following the tercentenary of Newton's birth in 1942. But Yahuda was also genuinely concerned about the material that he had collected and that remained in his hands until his death. He wrote to one correspondent: 'My opinion is that some rich Jew should be interested in the collection which is of great Biblical and religious interest for Protestants and Jews alike. All his treatises against the Catholic Church is still of actuality and they should be made public.' Despite a tone that was provoked by a real shortage of money, Yahuda was a serious student of the manuscripts that he bought and he did his best to analyse their content. After his death, they eventually found their way to the Jewish National and University Library in Jerusalem.

P. E. Spargo, 'Sotheby's, Keynes and Yahuda — the 1936 Sale of Newton's Manuscripts', in P.M. Harman and Alan E. Shapiro (eds), *The Investigation of Difficult Things* (Cambridge, 1992), pp. 115–34; King's College, Cambridge, Mss. PP58–9; Jewish National and University Library, Jerusalem, Mss. Yahuda 42 and 43.

71 *Library of Sir Isaac Newton. Presentation by the Pilgrim Trust to Trinity College, Cambridge, 30 October 1943*
(Cambridge, 1944)
Cambridge University Library, shelfmark Cam. d. 944.1.

After Newton's death, the books from his library had been listed and sold to John Huggins, Warden of the Fleet Prison, who seems to have bought them for his son Charles. They remained in the hands of his descendants and their heirs from the Musgrave family until 1920, when a significant portion was sold as part of the auction of Thame Park, Oxfordshire. Many of these books entered the trade and the London firm of Sotheran & Co. in particular acquired a large number of them. In 1928, Richard de Villamil announced that he had discovered the remainder of Newton's library among the books at Barnsley Park. In 1929, these books were also offered for sale by Sotheran & Co. They remained unsold, despite attempts to interest collectors like Keynes in purchasing them, until 1943. Then, in the wake of its purchase of Newton's birthplace, Woolsthorpe Manor, on behalf of the National Trust, the Pilgrim Trust was persuaded to buy the collection at the revised asking price of £5,000 and present it to Trinity College, Cambridge. The Master of Trinity, G.M. Trevelyan, took the lead in approaching the Pilgrim Trust for assistance, and accepted the books on behalf of the College on 30 October 1943.

John Harrison, *The Library of Isaac Newton* (Cambridge, 1978); H. Zeitlinger, 'A Newton Bibliography', in W. J. Greenstreet (ed.), *Isaac Newton 1642–1727* (London, 1927), pp. 148–70; R. de Villamil, *Newton: The Man* (London, [1931]).

72 CAMBRIDGE UNIVERSITY LIBRARY, MS. ADD. 8536, f. 2r
(figure 42)

J.M Keynes and A.S. Yahuda were responsible both for the amassing of substantial collections of Newton papers in the years following the Sotheby sale and for the beginning of the interpretation of those manuscripts. In 1942, Keynes was asked to prepare a brief talk about Newton's chemistry for an anniversary meeting of the Royal Society on 30 November to celebrate Newton's birth. He was subsequently asked to repeat it at Trinity College, Cambridge, in 1943 and a revised version was read by his brother, Geoffrey, on 17 July 1946 at the delayed public commemoration of Newton's tercentenary. This lecture summed up a

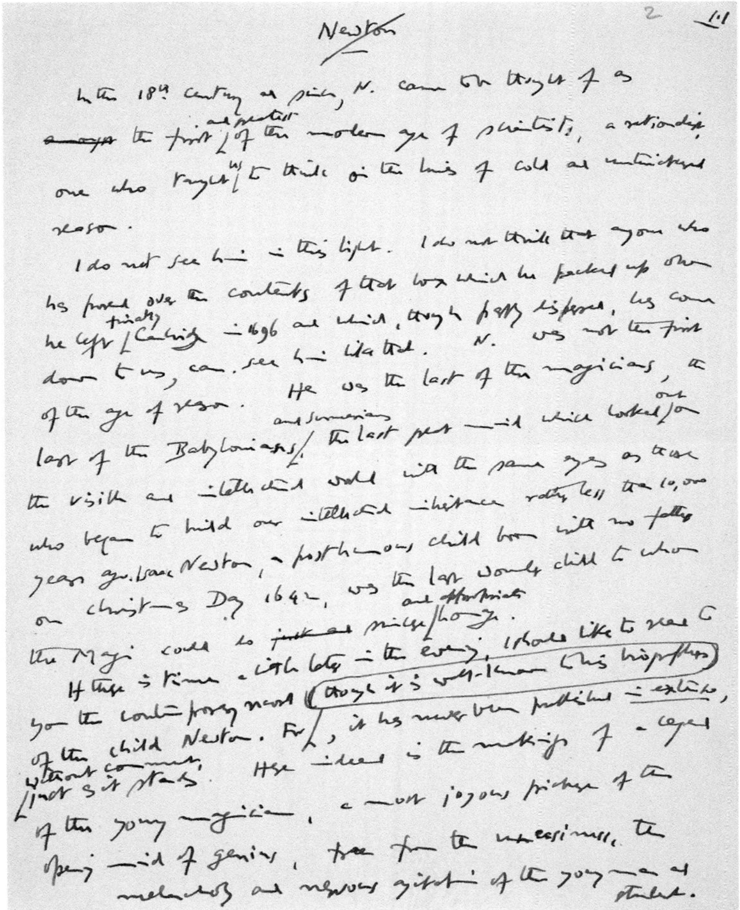
Newton

In the 18th Century as since, N. came to be thought of as the first and greatest of the modern age of scientists, a rationalist, one who taught us to think on the lines of cold and untinctured reason.

I do not see him in this light. I do not think that anyone who has pored over the contents of that box which he packed up when he left Cambridge finally in 1696 and which, though partly dispersed, has come down to us, can see him like that. N. was not the first of the age of reason. He was the last of the magicians, the last of the Babylonians and Sumerians, the last great mind which looked out on the visible and intellectual world with the same eyes as those who began to build our intellectual inheritance rather less than 10,000 years ago. Isaac Newton, a posthumous child born with no father on Christmas Day 1642, was the last wonder child to whom the Magi could do sincere and appropriate homage.

If there is time a little later in the evening, I should like to read you the contemporary record (though it is well-known to his biographers, it has never been published in extenso, without comment) of the child Newton. For, it is the makings of a legend. These ideas ... a most joyous picture of the young magician, the opening mind of genius, free from the uneasiness, the melancholy and nervous agitation of the young man student.

FIGURE 42
'The last of the magicians': Keynes sums up Newton's work, Cambridge University Library, Ms. Add. 8536, f. 2r.

change in Keynes' thinking about Newton. It also pointed to a development of the Sotheby sale that was to have long-term consequences for the understanding of Newton's work. In his talk, Keynes remarked that 'In the 18th Century as since, [Newton] came to be thought of as the first and greatest of the modern age of scientists, a rationalist, one who taught us to think on the lines of cold and untinctured reason... I do not see him in this light...[Newton] was not the first of the age of reason. He was the last of the magicians, the last of the Babylonians and Sumerians...'

Keynes' startling words represented a turning point. Since 1946, the study of Newton's manuscripts in all their forms has dominated the attempt to make sense of his ideas. Although Keynes' own interpretation now seems shockingly naïve, the papers that he helped to collect nevertheless make it possible to see Newton at work in all his guises for the first time.

John Maynard Keynes, *Essays in Biography*, ed. Geoffrey Keynes (London, 1951), pp. 310–23.

Presented to Cambridge University Library by Sir Geoffrey Keynes.